Managing Digital Records in Africa

Managing Digital Records in Africa draws on the research work of the InterPARES Trust (ITrust) project that investigated interrelated archival issues focusing on legal analysis, infrastructure, trust, authentication, and education within the African context.

This research-focused book provides a legal analysis and systematic assessment of how African institutions manage digital records in four countries (i.e., Botswana, Kenya, South Africa, and Zimbabwe). It also examines the extent to which records are managed using Internet-based applications, trust in such records, and digital record authentication to support the auditing process. Finally, it provides a curriculum analysis in digital records at institutions of higher learning in 38 African countries. The book's case studies illustrate the threads of discussion, which span the ITrust domains of legislation, infrastructure, authentication, trust, and education in archives and records management.

The book can be used as a premier reference source by private and public organizations, researchers, educators, archivists, records managers, and postgraduate students to make informed decisions about digital records, records management systems, cloud-based services, authenticating records, and identifying universities on the continent that offer archival programmes. The book may also find expression to practitioners in other fields such as law and auditing.

Mpho Ngoepe is a professor at the University of South Africa and the Director of the School of Arts. He was the Director of the InterPARES Trust project (2013–2018) for Team Africa.

Managing Digital Records in Africa

Edited by Mpho Ngoepe

Routledge
Taylor & Francis Group
LONDON AND NEW YORK

First published 2023
by Routledge
4 Park Square, Milton Park, Abingdon, Oxon OX14 4RN

and by Routledge
605 Third Avenue, New York, NY 10158

Routledge is an imprint of the Taylor & Francis Group, an informa business

© 2023 selection and editorial matter, Mpho Ngoepe; individual chapters, the contributors

The right of Mpho Ngoepe to be identified as the author of the editorial material, and of the authors for their individual chapters, has been asserted in accordance with sections 77 and 78 of the Copyright, Designs and Patents Act 1988.

With the exception of Chapters 1 and 5, no part of this book may be reprinted or reproduced or utilised in any form or by any electronic, mechanical, or other means, now known or hereafter invented, including photocopying and recording, or in any information storage or retrieval system, without permission in writing from the publishers.

Chapters 1 and 5 of this book are available for free in PDF format as Open Access from the individual product page at www.routledge.com. They have been made available under a Creative Commons Attribution-Non Commercial-No Derivatives 4.0 license.

Trademark notice: Product or corporate names may be trademarks or registered trademarks, and are used only for identification and explanation without intent to infringe.

British Library Cataloguing-in-Publication Data
A catalogue record for this book is available from the British Library

Library of Congress Cataloging-in-Publication Data
A catalog record for this book has been requested

ISBN: 978-1-032-06637-0 (hbk)
ISBN: 978-1-032-06638-7 (pbk)
ISBN: 978-1-003-20315-5 (ebk)

DOI: 10.4324/9781003203155

Contents

List of contributors	vii
Acknowledgements	viii
List of figures	ix
List of tables	x

Introduction: background, structure, and methodology   1
MPHO NGOEPE

1   Law and recordkeeping: a tale of four African countries   7
DARRA HOFMAN AND SHADRACK KATUU

2   Digital records infrastructure in Botswana, Kenya, South Africa, and Zimbabwe   49
FORGET CHATERERA-ZAMBUKO, MEHLULI MASUKU, AND SINDISO BHEBHE

3   Authentication of records for auditing processes   71
MPHO NGOEPE, JONATHAN MUKWEVHO, AND OLEFHILE MOSWEU

4   Trust dimensions of e-records in an African context: beyond statutory provisions   87
TRYWELL KALUSOPA AND TSHEPHO MOSWEU

5   Tapestry of the education and training landscape for archives and records management in Africa   99
SHADRACK KATUU

Epilogue 128
MPHO NGOEPE

*Annexure A Guidelines for authenticating digital records
   to support the audit process* 132
Index 137

Contributors

Sindiso Bhebhe, Department of Information Science, University of South Africa

Forget Chaterera-Zambuko, Records Management and Archival Science, Sorbonne University

Darra Hofman, School of Information, San Jose State University

Trywell Kalusopa, Department of Information Studies, University of Namibia

Shadrack Katuu, Department of Information Science, University of South Africa

Mehluli Masuku, Records Management and Archival Science, Sorbonne University

Olefhile Mosweu, Department of Information and Knowledge Management, University of Johannesburg

Tshepho Mosweu, Department of Information Science, University of Botswana and University of South Africa

Jonathan Mukwevho, Information and Knowledge Management Unit, Auditor General South Africa

Mpho Ngoepe, Department of Information Science, University of South Africa

Acknowledgements

Many people and organizations have significantly contributed to this publication. First, I am indebted to all of the InterPARES Team Africa's co-investigators and graduate research assistants from the University of British Columbia. Special mention should be made of the following: Anna Tidlund, Cathryn Crocker, Claire Williams, Darra Hofman, James Mark Penney, Marche Riley, Michelle Spelay, Rebecca Willmott, Robin Koning, Salma Berrada, Shadreck Bayane, Thinus Bekker, Vincent Mello, Lesetja Maraba, Nikiwe Momoti, Elsabe Maseh, Mangi Mulaudzi, Irene Moseti, Lorette Jacobs, Eric Boamah, Corine Rogers, and Luciana Duranti. The book would not have been published if the collaborators had not contributed. I am grateful to all of the authors who contributed chapters to this book. Finally, the University of South Africa, National Research Foundation, Auditor General of South Africa, Western Cape Provincial Archives, and Rand Water all provided support to the project, either in kind or financially. I also salute those I have consciously or unconsciously forgotten to mention.

Figures

1.1	Kenya's court structure	13
1.2	Hierarchy of laws	16
1.3	Predecessor institutions of the National Archives of Zimbabwe	26
2.1	ERP and ECM deployment by sector	56
2.2	Scope of ERP and ECM deployment	58
2.3	Participants by category	59
2.4	Cloud computing uses	60
2.5	Cloud computing service models used	62
2.6	Cloud computing deployment model	63
2.7	ERP modules deployed	65
5.1	South Africa's National Qualification Framework levels and qualification types	116
5.2	Kenya's National Qualification Framework levels and qualification types	117

Tables

1.1	Mixed law systems	9
2.1	Service providers per country	66
3.1	Evidence of lack of guidelines for authenticating digital records for auditing	82

Introduction
Background, structure, and methodology

Mpho Ngoepe

Background

This book is a result of eight years of enquiry into praxis-oriented acumens on the management of digital records in Africa by a new generation of records and archival scholars in Africa, conducted in conjunction with international peers. There have been similar efforts in the past, including the International Records Management Trust (2011, 2016); however, only a few of the contributors were from Africa, as revealed in the publications through the geographic and national provenance of the authors. In contrast, the challenges addressed in this book draw from the research of the International Project on Permanent Authentic Records in Electronic Systems (InterPARES) Trust project's Africa Team, therefore basing investigative motivation and processes entirely within the African continent. Essentially, this book addresses issues important for the continent in relation to digital records.

The management of records on the African continent has faced numerous challenges (Katuu, 2020). Mismanagement has, unfortunately, resulted in poor governance and accountability structures within governments (Mojapelo and Ngoepe, 2021). However, with the advent of technologies, there has been a belief that computerization would lead to a solution for record-keeping challenges (Nengomash, 2013). Although digital records have obvious advantages, studies in many regions of the world have shown that these records also come with challenges (Wilkins et al., 2009). Still, such studies are not widespread on the African continent (Katuu, 2012, 2020; Ngoepe, 2018).

More recent phenomena include the use of cloud computing, blockchain technologies, enterprise systems, enterprise and information architecture, as well as the utilization of artificial intelligence (AI) technologies in the management and preservation of records (Katuu, 2021; Modiba et al., 2019; Ngoepe and Mello, 2021). While it may not be widespread in Africa, the initiative is likely to mirror its global increase. Digital systems pose tremendous obstacles in the creation, maintenance, and preservation of records.

These issues, especially in Africa, are compounded by the lack of infrastructure, outdated legislation on managing digital records, and few universities offering archives and records management modules (Ngoepe, 2018; Stančić et al., 2019). Records managers, as well as archivists in Africa, have not fully engaged with these infinite challenges, which also include a lack of resources, skills, technology, and infrastructure.

Since 1998, the InterPARES project has been exploring theoretical, methodological, and practical issues, including a fixed documentation form and stable content for digital records, intellectual and digital components required to conceptualize digital records, and, ultimately, how to guarantee the trustworthiness of digital records over the long term (Duranti and Rogers, 2012). The first, second, and third phases of InterPARES took place from 1998 to 2012. The fourth phase, known as the InterPARES (IP) Trust, took place from 2013 to 2018. It explored how digital records were managed in both networked and Internet environments. The IP Trust's goal was to generate the theoretical and methodological frameworks that would support the development of integrated and consistent local, national, and international networks of policies, procedures, regulations, standards, and legislation concerning digital records entrusted to the Internet (Duranti, 2015). In the African context, the IP Trust project addressed three interrelated aims: (1) provide a systematic assessment of the extent to which institutions on the African continent were managing digital records; (2) examine the extent to which records were being managed using Internet-based applications and the risks that African institutions face in trying to follow the global trend; and (3) complete a curriculum review of digital records.

It is worth mentioning that, since the inception of the project, there has been no active engagement by African countries. Thus, while the InterPARES Project 3 (2013) did have an African team, research engagement was limited to a partnership through the International Records Management Trust. For the InterPARES Trust project, researchers from four African countries were involved: (1) Botswana; (2) Kenya; (3) South Africa; and (4) Zimbabwe. Observers were from Ghana, Mozambique, Namibia, Tanzania, Tunisia, and Zambia. Nonetheless, the project's case studies covered 38 African countries. The case studies investigated records and archive issues relating to infrastructure, auditing, education, legislation, and disruptive technology.

Structure

This book is based on the findings of the InterPARES Trust (Trust and Digital Records in an Increasingly Networked Society; ITrust) by Team Africa. Three interrelated issues are discussed. The first provides a legal analysis and systematic assessment of the extent to which institutions on the African continent are managing digital records. The second examines the extent to which records are being managed using Internet-based applications, trust in such records, and the authentication of digital records to support the auditing process. The third provides a curriculum review in digital records at institutions of higher learning in 38 countries in Africa. The three threads of discussion are exemplified in the book's five case studies that cut across the ITrust domains of control, authentication, trust, education, legislation, and infrastructure in archives and records management.

While there are similar categories of law impacting records and archives in Botswana, Kenya, South Africa, and Zimbabwe, the first chapter contends that each country's legal framework reflects its unique history and present. The chapter presents an overview of legal systems and sources of law to assist records and archives professionals in finding relevant laws and in understanding their obligations. It includes a discussion of the particulars of the law in each country that are most relevant to archives and records management. The chapter concludes that archives and records management professionals must equilibrate the need to fulfil the requirements of the law while serving the needs of the whole community to achieve broad representation towards a better future. A table of the examined laws is available on the InterPARES Trust Website.

Chapter 2 is also a product of a research alliance of researchers (from Botswana, Kenya, South Africa, and Zimbabwe) who conducted a separate harmonized study to ascertain the implementation of digital records infrastructure, particularly cloud computing, electronic content management, and enterprise resource planning (Chaterera et al., 2018; Kalusopa et al., 2018; Katuu, 2018; Moseti et al., 2018). In the context of the chapter, digital records infrastructure refers to the foundational tools and services needed to unlock acceptable records management practices for records held in digital spaces and electronic environments.

Chapters 3 and 4 focus on trust in digital records. Chapter 3, from a project which was commissioned by the Auditor General of South Africa, discusses authentication of records in the digital environment to support the audit process using the South African public sector in both municipalities and government departments. A checklist that auditors may use to judge the authenticity of digital records emanating from this study is available on the InterPARES Trust Website, while guidelines are in Annexure A of this book. Chapter 4 presents the trust dimension of e-records within the African context beyond legislative provisions. It is also based on case studies that examined the management of digital records in enterprise-wide systems in the public service in four countries, namely Botswana, Kenya, South Africa, and Zimbabwe.

Chapter 5 provides an overview of the education and training of archivists in Africa. It explores the historical context, including selection examples of national and regional efforts. The InterPARES Trust link provides an inventory of training institutions in 38 of the 54 countries on the African continent (Katuu et al., 2018).

Methodology

This research-focused book includes comparative case studies from several countries. Its combination of research was performed using primary and secondary sources. The final reports of the case studies were written in 2018. For this book, the team conducted follow-up surveys in 2021 to complete a comparative analysis of the data collected in all case studies. This initiative also ensured current, relevant empirical data. The sample size of the primary research differs between chapters. One case study instrument was used for each country case study. The data from this instrument were used to complete Chapters 2 and 4. Chapter 1 relied on literature review and document analysis covering a comparative analysis of archival legislation in Botswana, Kenya, South Africa, and Zimbabwe. Chapter 3 is a unique and commissioned case study on authentication. Primary documents, observation, system analysis, and focus groups were used during data gathering. Chapter 5 relied primarily on literature review and content analysis, especially websites of the universities.

After reading this book, practitioners, educators, students, decision makers, and stakeholders will be able to make informed choices regarding digital records, digital documents and records management systems, cloud-based services, authenticating records, identifying universities in the continent that offer archives and records management programmes, and recurriculation. Some of the benefits have already been reaped as universities in eastern and southern Africa started with the revision of archival programme curricula, including the University of Namibia, University of South Africa, and University of Eswatini (Ngoepe et al., 2022).

References

Chaterera, F., Masuku, M., Bhebhe, S., Ngoepe, M., Katuu, S. and Tidlund, A. (2018). *AF03 Investigating the management of digital records in enterprise-wide systems: Zimbabwe – final report*. Available at: https://interparestrust.org/assets/public/dissemination/AF03_Draft_FinalReport.pdf (Accessed 10 December 2021).

Duranti, L. (2015). *Overview of InterPARES trust: Work to date*. Available at: https://interparestrust.org/assets/public/dissemination/IPT_20150515_InternationalSymposium3_Duranti_InterPARESTrustOverview_Presentation.pdf (Accessed 18 April 2021).

Duranti, L. and Rogers, C. (2012). 'Trust in digital records: An increasingly cloudy legal area,' *Computer Law & Security Review*, 28 (5), pp. 522–531.

International Records Management Trust. (2011). *Managing records as reliable evidence for ICT/e-government and freedom of information in East Africa (2010–2011)*. London: International Records Management Trust. Available at: www.irmt.org/portfolio/managing-records-reliable-evidence-ict-e-government-freedom-information-east-africa-2010-%e2%80%93-2011 (Accessed 19 December 2021).

International Records Management Trust. (2016). *Education and training materials*. London: International Records Management Trust. Available at: www.irmt.org/education-and-training/education-and-training-2 (Accessed 19 December 2021).

InterPARES Trust. (2013). *Trust and digital records: Summary*. Vancouver: InterPARES Trust.

Kalusopa, T., Mosweu, T., Bayane, S., Ngoepe, M., Katuu, S., Penney, M. and Koning, R. (2018). *AF04 Enterprise digital records management in Botswana – final report*. Available at: https://interparestrust.org/assets/public/dissemination/AF04_FinalReport_July2018.pdf (Accessed 8 May 2021).

Katuu, S. (2012). 'Enterprise content management (ECM) implementation in South Africa,' *Records Management Journal*, 22 (1), pp. 37–56.

Katuu, S. (2018). *AF02 Managing records in networked environments: South Africa – final report*. Available at: https://interparestrust.org/assets/public/dissemination/AF02FinalReportMarch2018.pdf (Accessed 8 May 2021).

Katuu, S. (2020). 'Exploring the challenges facing archives and records management professionals in Africa: Historical influences, current developments and opportunities,' in R. Edmondson, L. Jordan and A. Prodan (eds.). *The UNESCO memory of the world programme*. Cham: Heritage Studies, Springer. https://doi.org/10.1007/978-3-030-18441-4_19.

Katuu, S. (2021). 'Trends in the enterprise resource planning market landscape,' *Journal of Information and Organizational Sciences*, 45, pp. 55–75.

Katuu, S., Ngoepe, M., Crocker, C., Spelay, M., Willmott, R., Berrada, S., Mosweu, O., Tidlund, A. and Penney, M. (2018). *AF01 Curriculum alignments at institutions of higher learning in Africa: preparing professionals to manage records created in networked environments*. Available at: https://interparestrust.org/assets/public/dissemination/AF01-FinalReport_1.pdf (Accessed 8 May 2021).

Modiba, T., Ngoepe, M. and Ngulube, P. (2019). 'Application of disruptive technologies to the management and preservation of records,' *Mousaion*, 37(1), pp. 1–14.

Mojapelo, M. and Ngoepe, M. (2021). 'Contribution of Auditor-General South Africa to records management in the public sector in South Africa,' *New Review for Information Network*, 26 (1–2), pp. 33–49.

Moseti, I., Maseh, E., Ngoepe, M., Katuu, S., Penney, M. and Hoffman, D. (2018). *AF05 Enterprise digital records management in Kenya – final report*. Available at: https://interparestrust.org/assets/public/dissemination/AF05FinalReport-March2018.pdf (Accessed 8 May 2021).

Nengomasha, C. T. (2013). 'The past, present and future of records and archives management in sub-Saharan Africa,' *Journal of the South African Society of Archivists*, 46, pp. 2–11.

Ngoepe, M. (2018). 'Playing catch-up: Africa's time to respond to grand societal challenges,' *Flash, ICA Newsletter*, 36 (September), pp. 18–19.

Ngoepe, M., Jacobs, L. and Mojapelo, M. (2022). 'Inclusion of digital records in the archives and records management curricula in a comprehensive open distance e-learning environment,' unpublished.

Ngoepe, M. and Mello, V. (2021). 'Integration of records management systems at a South African water utility company,' *Global Knowledge, Memory and Communication*, 70 (8/9), pp. 801–816.

Stančić, H., Ngoepe, M. and Mukwevho, J. (2019). 'Authentication,' in L. Duranti and C. Rogers (eds.). *Trusting records in the cloud*. London: Facet Publishing, pp. 135–154.

Wilkins, L., Swatman, P.M.C. and Holt, D. (2009). 'Achieved and tangible benefits: Lessons learned from a landmark EDRMS implementation,' *Records Management Journal*, 19 (1), pp. 37–53.

1 Law and recordkeeping

A tale of four African countries

Darra Hofman and Shadrack Katuu

Introduction

Archives and records management (ARM) professionals are inescapably entangled with the law. After all, the law may dictate what records must be created, their form, who may access them, their retention, and their eventual disposition. In each archival function, from selection and appraisal to referencing and access, the ARM professional must consider not only archival principles, but also legal requirements, putting an archivist without legal training in the position, for example, of determining what records fall within the scope of an access to information (ATI) request. This challenge is made more complex by the fact that the law rarely contemplates records as records, but rather as documents, information, and evidence. This chapter is based on an examination of major legal and regulatory instruments[1] related to records and archives management in Botswana, Kenya, South Africa, and Zimbabwe, undertaken to provide grounded, evidence-informed guidance for both practitioners and educators tasked with the responsibility of implementing recordkeeping. It should be noted, however, that a complete analysis of all the potential laws and regulations for each country was beyond the scope of this chapter. Furthermore, in those countries with elements of common law (discussed in greater detail *infra*), which include all of the countries in this study, judicial decisions ("case law") are of central importance in interpreting and implementing codified law; a full analysis of case law was also beyond the scope of this work. Nonetheless, this study identified major trends at the intersection of law and records, as well as archives, in the countries under study and may serve as a useful point of departure for ARM professionals in those countries and beyond for benchmarking.

Law as a system

"Those who have tried to define *law* agree only that no definition is fully satisfactory" (Garner, 1995, p. 503). However, a *legal system* "is a procedure

DOI: 10.4324/9781003203155-2

or process for interpreting and enforcing the law" (Cornell Law School, 2020), whatever the law may be. As will be discussed in more detail in "Law, archives, and colonialism," *infra*, the legal systems in this study, descended from various legal systems that differ in how they prioritize different sources of law, and in how they interpret and enforce the law. Knowing the system in which one operates, what sources of law it uses, and how it interprets and accords weight to those sources, is critical.

However, while ARM professionals must attend to the law as it is, it must be stated from the outset that the law is deeply problematic. The imposition of foreign legal systems "through colonialism, conquest, and some might add, neo-colonialism . . . created patterns of power, philosophy, and conduct, whose persistence has been aptly described as the coloniality of power" (Diala and Kangwa, 2019, pp. 190–191). Law's power is such that "colonial legal transplant in Africa was a comprehensive, self-replicating phenomenon, which was accompanied by radical socioeconomic changes that irrevocably affected the education, philosophy, religion, work, food, and dressing of Africans" (Diala and Kangwa, 2019, p. 190); the impact on recordkeeping is no less.

Legal systems which combine elements from multiple legal systems are referred to as "mixed legal systems," although there is disagreement among legal scholars as to precisely which systems are mixed. Perhaps unsurprisingly, scholarship on mixed legal systems originally centred on the mixing of European, and specifically English, common law and Roman civil law systems.

> Scholars in the "mixed jurisdiction" tradition, who follow the footsteps of early British comparatists . . . tend to restrict its scope to a single kind of hybrid where the most comparative research has been done – mixtures of common law and civil law. In that perspective the number of mixed systems in the field shrinks to fewer than twenty around the world. However, many scholars under the influence of legal pluralism . . . use a more expansive, factually oriented definition that enlarges the field and has no obvious limits.
>
> (Palmer, 2012, pp. 368–369)

Even in the narrowest – most Eurocentric – definition, many scholars consider Zimbabwe, South Africa, and Botswana as having mixed legal systems,[2] as their systems combine English common law and Roman-Dutch civil law. This developed due to the three countries' shared colonial history. Roman-Dutch law was introduced into the Dutch Cape Colony (which later became the Cape Colony) in 1652; therefore, Roman-Dutch law was received "directly" in South Africa, although English common law was significantly mixed. South Africa's law – and thus, the mixed system of civil and common law – was indirectly received into Botswana. The High Commissioners that the British had installed over Bechuanaland (now Botswana) and Southern Rhodesia (now Zimbabwe), which were often governed "by extending Proclamations designed for what is now South African to Botswana. The reception of the mixed system came through the High Commissioner's Proclamation of 10 June 1891," (Fombad, 2010, p. 6). These histories mean that, although all three countries have "mixed legal systems," each has developed uniquely.

As Fombad explains

> [w]hilst the reception of the common law and the civil law in South Africa can be described as direct it was only indirect in the other countries in the region, namely the former three High Commission Territories of Botswana, Lesotho and Swaziland, as well as Namibia and Zimbabwe ... this reception ... has influenced and continues to influence the quantum of each element of the mix that was received [and] also affects the way the different legal systems have evolved.
>
> (2010, p. 4)

Scholars estimate that there are fewer than 20 such mixed legal systems in the world (Palmer, 2012). However, as the legal pluralists correctly note, this Eurocentric view falsely posits that the world of laws is a "binary civil law/common law world" (Palmer, 2012, p. 378), when in reality, all legal systems "may be described as diversified blends." Understanding the elements of the legal system in which they work equips ARM professionals to navigate complex, often contradictory, landscapes of compliance, risk, and values. All four countries studied in this case have at least elements of common law, customary law, and indigenous law. Kenya, which arguably has the most clear-cut legal system of the four nations, nonetheless combines common law, customary and indigenous law, and Islamic law as reflected in Table 1.1.

Table 1.1 Mixed law systems

COUNTRY	MIXED LEGAL SYSTEM
Botswana	Civil law, customary law, and common law
Kenya	Common law, Muslim law, and customary law
South Africa	Civil law, customary law, and common law
Zimbabwe	Civil law, common law, and customary law

Source: (Palmer, 2012, pp. 379–382)

In the case of South Africa and Botswana, the legacy of multiple colonizers is a system that mixes common law, civil law, customary law, and indigenous law. South Africa and Botswana are, from even the most Eurocentric perspective, mixed law countries, because their legal systems inherited elements from both English common law and Roman-Dutch civil law, although, in reality, both countries' systems include elements of common, civil, customary, and indigenous law. Malila (2010, p. 71) notes that "Botswana, like other post-colonial transitional societies, is still faced with the continuing task of reconciling plural legal systems inherited from the formal colonial power at institutional, process, and value levels." South Africa has a "mixed legal system of predominantly English commercial and public law and Roman-Dutch private law, pervaded by the constitutional principles of personal freedom and the rule of law" (Van der Merwe, 2012, p. 113). As discussed in greater detail in "Case law," *infra*, English common law is a body of judge-made law in which previous cases on an issue are binding on future courts deciding the same issue. It should be noted, however, that common law jurisdictions still employ statutes to regulate their societies. Civil law jurisdictions, on the other hand, place primacy upon codes – the "Roman" in Roman-Dutch refers to the Justinian Code, which forms the basis of European civil law. In civil law systems, case law does not serve as a binding precedent for future cases.

Van der Merwe's (2012) explanation of South African law also raises the important distinction between *public* and *private* law. Public law is that which regulates relationships between individuals and the state, and includes criminal, constitutional, and administrative law. Private law, by contrast, regulates relationships between individuals, and includes contract and tort law. Confusingly, some common law jurisdictions such as the United States and Canada refer to private law as "civil law." Therefore, in South Africa, commerce and relationships between the individual and the state are primarily controlled and can be changed by judge-made law, while the relationships between private individuals are still primarily controlled by legal codes. Within private law, a further category of *personal law* exists, which is "the law that governs a given person in family matters" (Garner, 1995, p. 655). As Palmer (2012, p. 377) writes, "Rarely has any people willingly given up its own personal law or voluntarily accepted someone else's," and it's in the area of personal law where "customary law" is most often recognized. Thus, personal law is the legal area in which precolonial culture and practice are most likely to persist, and records related to personal law may provide a more representative picture of a nation and its peoples.

Zimbabwe faces unusual challenges in the regulation of its records management due to its unique colonial history (Ncube, 2016). Like many colonized nations, Zimbabwe has oral indigenous recordkeeping traditions that were at odds with the written traditions of settler recordkeeping and government (Chaterera, 2016). However, Zimbabwe, unlike many other nations, was not a full British colony, but was rather under the rule of the British South Africa Company; its rule by a private company meant that its records throughout the colonial period did not belong to the government (either of Zimbabwe or of the United Kingdom), but to a private company based in London. The governmental – and public records – context and challenges in Zimbabwe have largely been in response to the country's struggles with the legacies of colonization.

All four of the nations in this study, continue to bear the marks of colonialism in their legal and bureaucratic systems. Thus, while ARM professionals in Botswana, Kenya, South Africa, and Zimbabwe share issues with archivists in Belgium and Canada, such as custody and control over digital, and especially cloud-based records, they also face challenges that are unique to their contexts. Furthermore, solutions developed for Western nations facing novel records-related challenges, such as data-mining – including access to information and data protection laws – may be inadequate or ill-suited for recordkeeping in Africa. For example, with regard to access to information, the dominant scholarly narrative focuses on legislation as the "solution" to the problem of information accessibility and transparency. This narrative paints African countries and recordkeepers as "failed," without examining the "political, social, administrative, and economic conditions that prevail" (Calland and Diallo, 2013, p. 2) in those countries. Similarly, the legalistic approach that treats data protection laws as the solution to massive data collection and surveillance fails to recognize the colonial socioeconomic dimensions and power disparities ("digital colonialism") at play when Western technology companies extract and exploit data from African people (Coleman, 2019).

Given the mixed nature of the legal systems, there are four primary sources of law in the countries under study: constitutions, statutes and regulations, case law, and customary and indigenous law.

Sources of law

Constitution

"Constitutionalism is the idea that governmental authority is conferred and defined by the people through a fundamental law known as the Constitution" (Diala and Kangwa, 2019, p. 189). A constitution, "a written document containing the principles of governmental organization of a nation" (Garner, 1995, p. 208), is the "supreme law in a country to which all other laws must adhere" (Clegg et al., 2016, p. 2). This means that any proposed (or even passed) law that contradicts the constitution is *unconstitutional*, and therefore unlawful. As will be discussed in greater detail *infra*, a number of the major themes in the law impacting ARM work are embedded in countries' constitutions. For example, both Botswana and South Africa have a constitutional right of access to information (Adeleke, 2013). However, scholars such as Darch (2013), Diala and Kangwa (2019), and Khan (2020) argue that constitutionalism is deeply problematic in post-colonial states in Africa.

Statutes and regulations

A statute is "a legislative act that the state gives the force of law" (Garner, 1995, p. 829). Statutes are often called "laws" in the lay vernacular. Statutes obtain their authority from the constitution, which "authorizes the legislature to enact it" (Clegg et al., 2016, p. 9). In some countries, such as Kenya, the constitution will divide law-making authority between different legislatures, such as the national and county governments. Regulations, in turn, "are issued under the authority of a statute by a division of the government or by a special body" (Clegg et al., 2016, p. 2). Most of the laws dealt with in this chapter are *omnibus* laws, or laws that address an issue regardless of sector. However, ARM professionals must also be aware of the *sectoral* laws that may apply to their organization, for example, banking laws that impose particular information security requirements or health care laws that impose specific privacy requirements.

Case law

In a number of countries, especially those previous colonized by England, *case law*, or the body of law made up of judicial decisions, is an important source of law. Such systems, called common law systems, treat judgments as one of the most important sources of binding the law under the doctrine of precedent, called *stare decisis*, which means "let decided things stand" (Garner, 1995, p. 825). Under *stare decisis*, court decisions become *precedent* and bind the court in future cases on the same matter. Thus, in a common law system, if the interpretation or application of a particular law is in dispute, it is brought before a court with jurisdiction over the matter. Once that court makes a decision (for example, if the court holds that the Public Officer Ethics Act applies to government archivists and records managers), that decision applies to all future decisions in that court and all courts beneath it. A court may only make decisions on cases that fall within that court's jurisdiction; jurisdiction can be limited either geographically or functionally.

Jurisdiction is given in the constitution and other legislation. Thus, the Supreme Court of Kenya, for example, has jurisdiction geographically over the whole of Kenya; it also has appellate jurisdiction over all disputes being brought up from the Court of Appeal (see Figure 1.1 for Kenya's court structure). The Supreme Court also has original jurisdiction over disputes concerning presidential elections, which means that disputes concerning presidential elections are initially brought before the Supreme Court, as opposed to being brought up on appeal. Most cases, however, will begin somewhere near the bottom of the hierarchy, and be "brought up" to higher levels of court through the appellate process.

Thus, a decision by the Supreme Court will be binding upon all courts of lower jurisdiction. On the other hand, a decision by the High Court is *not* binding on the Court of Appeal or the Supreme Court, because the High Court is a lower court. Thus, a particular question will (in most cases), be brought before a low-level court (such as a Magistrate Court). If that court's decision is not appealed, it will stand as a binding decision for that court.

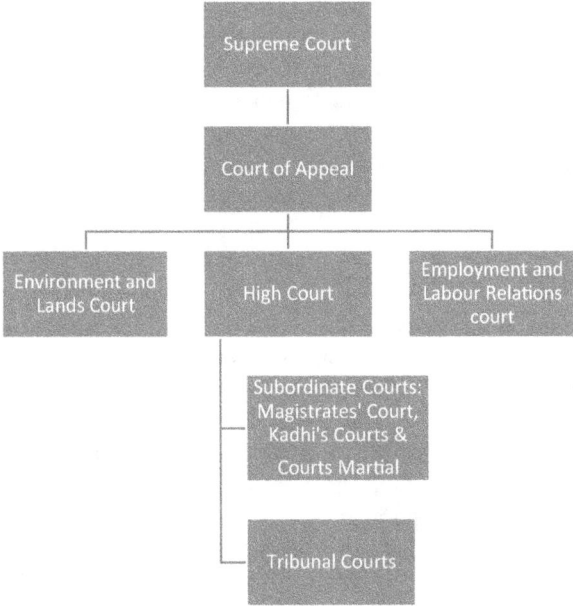

Figure 1.1 Kenya's court structure

Long Description: Figure showing Kenya's courts in hierarchical order. Supreme Court at the top, Court of Appeal below it, High Court below it with Environmental and Lands Court as well as Employment and Labour Relations Courts at the same level. Below the High Court are Subordinate Courts i.e. Magistrates' Court, Kadhi's Courts and Courts Martial. Below subordinate courts are Tribunal Courts

Source: (Kenya Judiciary, 2021)

If it is appealed up to the High Court, the High Court's decision will be binding on the High Court *and* the lower-level courts (i.e., the Magistrate Courts) in the future. As an example, the High Court held in *High Court of Kenya Petition No. 43 of 2012, Famy Care Limited vs. Public Procurement Administrative Review Board & Another [2012]* that "1) The right to information is only enjoyable by Kenyan Citizens, and not foreign citizens [and] **2)** The right to information is enjoyable by **natural Kenya Citizens** and not **Kenyan juridical persons** such as corporations, or associations" (Georgiadis, 2012 emphasis in original). This holding could be overturned by a superior court (the Court of Appeal or the Supreme Court) or by the High Court in a later case. It could also be overturned by legislation (for example, the Access to Information Act could have stated that it applied the right of access to all citizens, natural and juridical, or to all persons, citizen and non-citizen). Unless and until the holding is overturned, however, it is considered "good law" and binding on the High Court and all lower courts.

Furthermore, a decision even by the highest court of Zimbabwe, the Supreme Court, is not binding on any court in Kenya, because Zimbabwe's courts (and legislature) have no jurisdiction over Kenya. However, decisions from a court without binding authority may be used as *persuasive* precedent, one that courts are not obligated to follow, but may consider. Binding precedent is one of the distinguishing characteristics of a common law system; precedent in civil law systems is only persuasive.

Customary law and indigenous law

Finally, it would be remiss to discuss sources of law without discussing customary law and indigenous law, which are related but far from the same thing. *Customary law* is defined as:

> Practices and beliefs that are so vital and intrinsic a part of a social and economic system that they are treated as if they were laws. *Customary law* is handed down for many generations as unwritten law, though it is usually collected finally in a written code.
>
> (Garner, 1995, p. 241)

Diala and Kangwa (2019), however, make the important point that "customary law" in African nations is not the indigenous law that existed prior to colonization. As they explain, "indigenous laws are oral precolonial norms which people observe in their ancient forms, while customary laws are adaptations of precolonial norms to socioeconomic changes" (Diala and Kangwa, 2019, p. 197). Furthermore, "most indigenous laws have transformed into customary laws through people's adaptations to legal, economic, religious, and globalisation-fuelled changes in intersecting social fields" (Diala and Kangwa, 2019, p. 189). Given the immense dislocations in socioeconomic life imposed by both colonialism and industrial capitalism, Diala and Kangwa (2019, p. 200) argue that adhering to the letter of indigenous laws would be problematic, for the laws existed to uphold community values in a particular context, and "would have changed with or without the influence of colonial rules."

Islamic law

As noted *supra*, Kenya has an additional source of law, Islamic law (*shariah*), which governs some questions of personal law among Muslim Kenyans through courts known as Kadhi's courts. This is also a legacy of colonization. In the late 19th century, when Kenya and other parts of East Africa were placed under either British or German protection, there was a treaty between the Europeans and the Sultan of Zanzibar – the previous sovereign – to have the coastal strip of Tanzania and Kenya respect the Islamic judicial system (Chesworth, 2010). "The colonial administration set up a tri-partite legal system: common law (colonial) courts, Kadhi's courts, and customary courts," (Wario, 2013, p. 153). As can be seen from the chart in Figure 1.1, the Khadi's courts remain subordinate to the common law courts (Supreme Court, Court of Appeal, and High Court of Kenya). The Khadi's courts have limited jurisdiction, being restricted by the Constitution of Kenya to "determination of questions of Muslim law relating to personal status, marriage, divorce and inheritance in proceedings in which all the parties profess the Muslim religion and submit to the jurisdiction of the Kadhi's courts" (Republic of Kenya, 2010, Article 170, Section 5). Although the Khadi's courts existed in the Coastal Strip "much earlier than the period of establishment of British colonization" (Wario, 2013, p. 153), the imposition of the colony extended to the courts beyond the Coastal Strip and the lands subject to the rule of the Sultanate of Zanzibar. The status of the Kadhi's courts was an important point of debate in the adoption of the new constitution, with "debates about the courts . . . embroiled in discussing earlier protracted clashes over resources such as land, economic opportunities, political leadership, and conflicts over control of educational institutions and boundary disputes" (Wario, 2013, p. 164). For recordkeepers in Kenya, questions of Islamic law are likely to arise only in the context of records related to personal law, for example, matters of marriage, divorce, and inheritance (Osiro, 2013). As Wario (2013, p. 157) rightly reminds us, "conflict, or the lack of it, is usually shaped by historical and socio-economic circumstances." Understanding the law of recordkeeping in Africa necessitates tracing several sources of laws that arose in a great

16 *Darra Hofman and Shadrack Katuu*

diversity of historical and socio-economic circumstances. For ARM professionals, analysis of both the letter and the spirit of the law may help in the resolution of tricky cases, weighing up what must be done in the name of compliance versus what can or should be done in furtherance of the institution and/or the profession's values.

Hierarchy of laws

It should also be noted that laws are hierarchical – they apply as long as they do not conflict with a law of higher precedence. The broad rights and principles in the Constitution are implemented through statutes, which, in turn, are fleshed out through regulations, and regulations are put into practice through policies and standards. Therefore, in the context of South Africa, the National Archives Act is only valid law if it does not conflict with the Constitution, and the National Archives Regulations are valid law if they do not conflict with either the National Archives Act or the Constitution. There are also a number of government publications (such as the National Archive's Records Management Policy Manual and Advisory Publications) which do *not* have the force of law but could be offered as evidence of the correct interpretation of a law. In the illustration in Figure 1.2, blue sources are law and red sources are not.

Attention must also be paid to the language of the laws themselves – an act will often explicitly state its relationship to other acts. For example, in Kenya, the Access to Information Act (No. 31 of 2016) states that "Nothing in this Act shall limit the requirement imposed under this Act or any other written law on a public entity or a private body to disclose information" (Section 4(5)); thus, disclosure requirements in other legislation, such as the

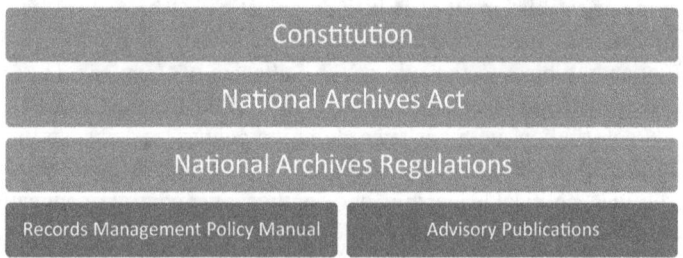

Figure 1.2 Hierarchy of laws

Long Description: Graph showing hierarchy of laws with the Constitution at the top, then the National Archives Act, National Archives regulations and below that two sets of regulations at the same level: Records Management Policy Manual and Advisory Publications

Companies Act, Cap. 486, should not be limited by the Access to Information Act, even if the Access to Information Act would seem to imply otherwise. Sometimes, however, the law does not explicitly address conflicts between acts. Where acts contradict each other, a prudent approach is to adhere to the act with the higher standard until such a time as the conflict is brought before the courts to be resolved (thus, if one act prescribes a minimum five-year retention period, whereas another seems to prescribe seven years for the same type of record, the safest course is to retain those records for seven years). Finally, it must be remembered that policies and standards such as the National Policy on Records Management, while very helpful, are not law and can be changed at any time by their creating bodies.

Interpretation and enforcement of law

One of the great challenges in law is interpreting the law. With regard to statutes, there are a number of rules of interpretation that lawyers and judges rely on; however, those rules are also subject to interpretation. Hon. Malcolm Wallis, Judge of the Supreme Court of Appeal of South Africa, writes that when he was in law school,

> The rule, so we were told, was that statutes should be given their literal meaning, but that courts could depart from this if the literal meaning would result in an absurdity. In a country where much of the legislation affecting the population seemed absurd, this was difficult to comprehend, even in those far-off times.
>
> (Wallis, 2019, p. 2)

Perhaps it is unsurprising, then, that Judge Wallis wrote the decision that expanded the rules of statutory interpretation:

> The present state of the law can be expressed as follows: Interpretation is the process of attributing meaning to the words used in a document, be it legislation, some other statutory instrument, or contract, having regard to the context provided by reading the particular provision or provisions in the light of the document as a whole and the circumstances attendant upon its coming into existence. Whatever the nature of the document, consideration must be given to the language used in the light of the ordinary rules of grammar and syntax; the context in which the provision appears; the apparent purpose to which it is directed, and the material known to those responsible for its production. Where more than one meaning is possible each possibility must be weighed in the light of all these factors. The process is objective,

not subjective. A sensible meaning is to be preferred to one that leads to insensible or unbusiness-like results or undermines the apparent purpose of the document. Judges must be alert to, and guard against, the temptation to substitute what they regard as reasonable, sensible or business-like for the words actually used. To do so in regard to a statute or statutory instrument is to cross the divide between interpretation and legislation; in a contractual context it is to make a contract for the parties other than the one they in fact made. The "inevitable point of departure is in the language of the provision itself", read in context and having regard to the purpose of the provision and the background to the preparation and production of the document.

(Natal Joint Municipal Pension Fund v Endumeni Municipality, 2012 4 SA 593 (SCA), p. 603–4)

In other words, laws should be interpreted according to their *plain language*, taking into account the context in which the language appears, its purpose, and the context of its creation, with a focus on the law itself, and not the outcome that seems most sensible to the interpreter. In the countries in this study, statutory law co-exists with case law, which, for example, may provide clarity on the meaning of the terms or the scope of the law. Thus, an ARM professional looking to adhere to access to information requirements in South Africa would have constitutional, statutory, and case law to consider together, to understand the full scope of their obligations.

Law, archives, and colonialism

The law-archives interface in the four countries studied has been indelibly shaped by colonialism and by European legal imperialism. As Khan (2020, p. 1) writes, "Colonialism constructed legal identities and subjects, many of which found their way into post-independence constitutional frameworks [. . . leading] to the legacy of colonisation continuing." Katuu (2020, p. 276), discussing the challenges facing ARM professionals in Africa, reminds us that,

> Tracing of different nations throughout the course of the colonial and post-colonial periods is critical in setting the stage for any discussions on current developments. . . . The socio-political history of any nation has a huge impact on the juridical and administrative structure, which forms the overriding context within which ARM professions have to work.

Part of the legacy of colonialism is that the legal systems of previously colonized countries often contain elements of the legal systems of multiple colonizers. Based on their unique pre-colonial, colonial, and post-colonial histories, each of the countries under study have developed a legal system combining different systems, including customary law, indigenous law, English common law, Roman-Dutch civil law, and, in the case of Kenya, Islamic law, see, for example (Palmer, 2012). Just as colonizers imposed different legal traditions, they also imposed different recordkeeping traditions; speaking of the English and French, Katuu (2020, p. 279) notes that "the recordkeeping traditions from the two major colonial powers on the continent were very different." Furthermore, as discussed in greater detail in the section on customary law, *supra*, each of the countries studied is home to a number of people and cultures who had their own legal systems, cultural values, and norms prior to colonization. European systems of law and records as well as archives were not written on a blank slate, but "coercively changed the normative behaviours of Africans. . . [leading to the creation of customary law that] occurred in the context of dissonance between indigenous and state laws" (Diala and Kangwa, 2019, p. 190). Thus, ARM professionals in the countries studied must function in what may be termed as mixed legal systems which impose unique challenges as noted earlier in this chapter.

National archives and archives law

All four of the countries in this study have National Archives, a national archives law, and other laws directly on the issue of recordkeeping. Even for ARM professionals outside the national archives, the national archives law can provide insight into such matters as how the country's law views the evidentiary character of records, the nature of the country's approach to digital records, and how the country draws the boundary between public and private records.

Botswana

The Botswana National Archives and Records Services (BNARS) was established in 1967 and is governed by the National Archives and Records Services (NARS) Act of 1978 as amended in 2007. Before this Act was enacted, the Botswana National Archives operated through a presidential directive (Mosweu and Simon, 2018, p. 72). The NARS Act provides that:

The functions of the National Archives and Records Services shall be –

(a) To provide records and information management service to government agencies; and
(b) To collect, preserve, and access the nation's documentary heritage.

(Botswana, 1978 Section 3A)

However, neither the statute nor its attendant regulations further address electronic records directly, which goes against the assertion that "it is advisable to make clear that the law applies to archival documents irrespective of their physical forms" (Mosweu and Simon, 2018, p. 87). Legislation does not exist in a vacuum; the Electronic Evidence (Records) Act (No. 13 of 2014) and Electronic Communications and Transactions Act (No. 14 of 2014) further support the treatment of electronic records as legally authentic records and provide some guidance as to what is necessary to ensure the ongoing availability and trustworthiness of electronic records (Botswana, 2014a, 2014b). The Electronic Records (Evidence) Act (No. 13 of 2014) and Electronic Communications and Transactions Act (No. 14 of 2014) work together to provide for the legal admissibility and authenticity of electronic records and to facilitate electronic transactions. "Nothing in the rules of evidence shall apply to deny the admissibility of an electronic record in evidence on the sole ground that it is an electronic record" (Botswana, 2014b Section 5(1)). Furthermore, the Electronic Records (Evidence) Act states that "evidence may be presented in respect of any standard, procedure, usage, or practice concerning the matter in which the electronic records are to be recorded or stored," opening the door for consideration of electronic recordkeeping standards (Botswana, 2014b ss. 10).

The *Electronic Communications and Transactions Ac*t gives legal recognition to electronic communications outside the confines of evidence law. "Subject to the provisions of this Act, information shall not be denied legal effect, validity, or enforcement solely on the grounds that (a) it is in the form of an electronic communication" (Botswana, 2014a ss. 3). The Act also states that an electronic writing is sufficient to meet a legal requirement to give information in writing (Botswana, 2014a ss. 4). The Act also provides that retention of electronic records is sufficient to meet legal retention obligations (Botswana, 2014a ss. 9), and that secure electronic signatures are sufficient for notarization and/or verification requirements (Botswana, 2014a ss. 11). When read in the context of these two acts, one can discern a framework for the authorized use of electronic records, even if the archival legislation does not expressly provide for it.

Kenya

The laws addressing archives and records management in Kenya are numerous and diverse. For example, while one would not typically think of the penal code when considering recordkeeping, Cap. 63, Sec. 133 imposes criminal penalties for anyone who destroys or even "fails to preserve" any document that falls within a broad swath of "statutory documents" without the authority to do. While it is beyond the scope of this chapter to discuss all the laws that regulate recordkeeping, it does try to address the major laws (the Constitution, National Archives Act, and the freedom of information, data protection, and information security laws) that address all public sector recordkeeping. This chapter also does not address county level law. While it is possible that some county level law addresses records management within the areas of power assigned to the counties under Schedule Four of the Constitution, such application would be limited to that particular subject matter within that particular county – the law in Mombasa regarding required records in a childcare facility may well differ from those of Kwale. However, Kenya's government is strongly central; all powers not specifically devolved to the counties in the Constitution belong to the national government, and the national government may regulate within those areas devolved to the counties through an Act of Parliament.

Kenya's national archival law is the *Public Archives and Documentation Service Act*, Cap. 19 (Act No. 2 of 1990). This Act requires that there be "established, constituted and maintained a public department to be known as the Kenya National Archives and Documentation Service" (Section 3(1)), and places upon the director of that service the responsibility for "proper housing, control, and preservation of all public archives and public records" (Section 3(2)). Public archives are defined as "all public records and other records which are housed or preserved in the national archives or which are deemed to be part of the public archives" (Section 2). Public records are defined in the Schedule, Section 2:

1. The records of any Ministry or Government Department and of any commission, office, board or other body or establishment under the government or established by or under an Act of Parliament: Provided that nothing referred to in this paragraph shall include the records of the public trustee or of the registrar-general relating to individual trusts or estates.
2. The records of the High Court and of any other court or tribunal.
3. The records of Parliament and of the Electoral Commission.
4. The records of any local authority or other authority established for local government purposes.

Thus, those records which fall within the purview of the National Archives and Documentation Service include, but are not limited to, public records. In particular, the director is empowered to acquire "any document, book, record, or other material of any description or historical or other value, or any copy or replica thereof which he considers should be added to the public records" (Section 4(1)(h)). It is also worth noting from the definitions section that "'records' includes not only written records, but records conveying information by any means whatsoever" (Section 2).

For records managers and other custodians of public records, it is important to note that

> It shall be the duty of every person responsible for, or having the custody of any public records to afford to the Director or any officer of the Service authorized by him reasonable access to such public records and appropriate facilities for the examination and selection thereof, and to comply without any undue delay with any lawful directions given by the Director or such officer concerning the assemblage, safe keeping and preservation of such public records or of the transfer of any such public records to the national archives to form part of the public archives.
>
> (Section 4(2))

Thus, custodians of public records have a significant potential obligation to the National Archives and Documentation Service. The Act also creates several offences for willfully destroying or disposing of, defacing, mutilating, or damaging public archives (those records that have passed the archival threshold into the national archives), except in such cases where the director has authorized such destruction (Section 8).

Records in the custody of the public archives are accorded all legal respect. In such cases where public records are required to be kept in or produced from legal custody, they remain in valid legal custody if transferred to the public archives (Section 10). Furthermore, certified copies of records from the public archives are admissible as evidence "in any proceedings" in which the original record would have been admissible (Section 11). Rules for the disposal of records belonging to or being in the custody of the courts or the registrar-general may be made in consultation with the director of the Kenya National Archives and Documentation Service, subject to the provisions of the Public Archives and Documentation Service Act, Cap. 19 (Records Disposal Act, Cap. 14, Section 2).

The Kenya Information and Communications Act, 2009, establishes and empowers the Communications Authority of Kenya to "licence and regulate postal, information and communication services" (Section §5(1)). Part of that broad mandate includes facilitating, promoting, and fostering the development of electronic transactions and commerce (Section 83C). In line with those goals, this act provides for legal recognition of electronic records, stating that,

> Where any law provides that information or other matter shall be in writing then, notwithstanding anything contained in such law, such requirement shall be deemed to have been satisfied if such information

or matter is – (a) rendered or made available in an electronic form; and (b) accessible so as to be usable for a subsequent reference.

(Section 83G)

The *Kenya Information and Communications Act*, 2009, provides standards for the retention of electronic records, requiring that:

> Where any law provides that documents, records or information shall be retained for any specific period, then that requirement shall be deemed to have been satisfied where such documents, records or information are retained in electronic form if:
>
> (a) the information contained therein remains accessible so as to be usable for subsequent reference
> (b) the electronic record is retained in the format in which it was originally generated, sent or received or in a format that can be demonstrated to represent accurately the information originally generated, sent or received
> (c) the details that will facilitate the identification of the original destination, date and time of dispatch or receipt of such electronic record are available in the electronic record.

(Section 83H)

Under Article 83I, an electronic record is sufficient where the law requires that records or information be retained in their original form, as long as there are adequate safeguards of the integrity and reliability of that record. Article 83P provides for legal recognition of electronic signatures. Article 83S empowers government agencies to utilize electronic records to meet a variety of administrative needs, including delivery of public goods and services, the filing of forms and applications, the issuances of grants and permits, and the receipt of payment.

South Africa

The National Archives and Records Service of South Africa Act (hereafter, National Archives Act or NARS Act) sets out a sophisticated system of archival control and responsibility, anchored in the National Archives and the National Archivist. The Act vests ultimate accountability for "the proper management and care of public records in the custody of governmental bodies," as well as for the non-public record of enduring value, in the National Archivist (Section 13). This Act also empowers the National Archives to promulgate "regulations as to the management and care of public records in the custody of governmental bodies" (Section 13(3)); such regulations have been issued and provide further detail and direction as to how the National Archives and governmental bodies shall perform functions such as records transfer and disposal, appraisal, and classification. Both the act and regulations have force of law, as far as they do not conflict with the Constitution (or, in the case of the regulations, they do not conflict with the act). The specific accountabilities of the National Archives include all of the traditional archival functions: appraisal and acquisition, arrangement and description, retention and preservation, management and administration, and reference and access. The act and regulations authorize liberal delegation on the part of the National Archivist and leave the National Archives significant liberty in how they meet their responsibilities (for example, the regulations require only that public bodies use an approved classification system; they do not dictate the required classification system). Ultimately, the National Archives Act "provides the anchor for the management of records, including digital records" (Katuu and Ngoepe, 2015, p. 61).

Mosweu and Simon (2018, p. 85) compare Botswana's archival legislation to the National Archives Act, which outlines nine functions of the National Archives. One function which South African legislation makes explicit, as Mosweu and Simon (2018) discuss at some length, is to "collect non-public records with enduring value of national significance which cannot be more appropriately preserved by another institution" (South Africa, 1996 Section 3 (d)). However, while the primary Botswanan legislation does not directly provide for such acquisitions, Part VI: General ss 2728, Section 28 of the National Archives and Records Services Regulations does provide for the donation of such archives, with Schedule 1, Form D of those regulations providing a Deed of Gift for such acquisitions. Furthermore, South Africa's (1996 Chapter 59:04) NARS Act empowers the director of the National Archives to, "on behalf of the government, acquire by purchase, donation, bequest or otherwise any private archive which in the opinion of the director is or is likely to be of enduring or historical value." Thus, the legislation clearly contemplates, even if it does not directly specify, acquisition of private archives as part of the mandate of the National Archives and Records Service. The two functions specified are incredibly broad – they could be summarized as current records management and archives management – and arguably contemplate the narrower functions of the South African legislation within their sweep. The powers given to the director (ss. 5 et seq.) comprise the full range of archival functions, including appraisal and acquisition, arrangement and description, retention and preservation, management and administration, and reference and access. The Minister also has broad powers under the statute to bring records within the purview of the National Archives and Records Service, being empowered to "declare any public body, corporation, society, association, institution, organization or any body of persons, whether incorporated or not, to be a prescribed body for the purposes of this Act and the documents of such body shall be public records" (South Africa, 1996 Chapter 59:04, ss. 7).

The NARS Act also accords legal authenticity to records within the custody of the National Archives and Records Service, providing:

> A copy of or extract from any record in the National Archives and Records Services or place of deposit purporting to be duly certified as true and authentic by the Director, or by any authorized officer or by the custodian of the public archives in any place of deposit where such record is kept, and authenticated by having impressed thereon the official seal of the National Archives and Records Services or of the place of deposit, shall be admissible in evidence if the original record would have been admissible in evidence in any proceedings.
> (South Africa, 1996 Chapter 59:04, ss. 17)

Mosweu and Simon (2018) fairly raise the lack of clarity within the NARS Act regarding electronic records. The statute provides a definition of "records" that clearly intends to include digital as well as paper records:

> **"records"** (emphasis in original) includes any electronic records, manuscript, newspaper, picture, painting, document, register, printed material, book, map, plan, drawing, photograph, negative and positive pictures, photocopy, microfilm, cinematograph film, video tape, magnetic tape, gramophone record or other transcription of language, picture or music, recorded by any means capable of reproduction and regardless of physical form and characteristics.
> (South Africa, 1996 Chapter 59:04, ss. 2(c))

Zimbabwe

The National Archives of Zimbabwe was originally established during the 1930s under the colonial government. However, this statement is a vast oversimplification of the complex history of those archives. As noted *supra*, during the colonial period, Zimbabwe was under the rule of the British South Africa Company. Among records being expropriated to London, and those within the country being "not properly cared for and ... haphazardly destroyed ... Zimbabwe lost some crucial part of its documentary heritage" (Chaterera, 2016, p. 119). The National Archives of Rhodesia (the country now known as Zimbabwe was "Southern Rhodesia" during the colonial period, while Zambia was "Northern Rhodesia") was created by an Act of Parliament (the Parliament of the United Kingdom) in 1935. Chaterera (2016, p. 119) explains the subsequent development of and changes in the composition of these archives:

> in 1946 . . . the Southern Rhodesian government archives took responsibility in Northern Rhodesia and Nyasaland [now Malawi] to form what came to be known as the Central African Archives [citation omitted]. In 1953, three Southern African territories named Southern Rhodesia (Zimbabwe), Norther Rhodesia (Zambia) and Nyasaland (Malawi) came together to form a federation that came to be known as the Central African Federation (CAF) . . . which resulted in the Central African Archives changing its name to the National Archives of Rhodesia and Nyasaland and further renamed the National Archives of Rhodesia in 1963 after the federation had dissolved. The name changed to the National Archives of Zimbabwe in 1980 when the country achieved independence.

The National Archives of Zimbabwe, then, are inextricably bound to the colonial history of both Zimbabwe and its neighbouring nations (see Figure 1.3 for predecessor institutions of the national Archives of Zimbabwe).

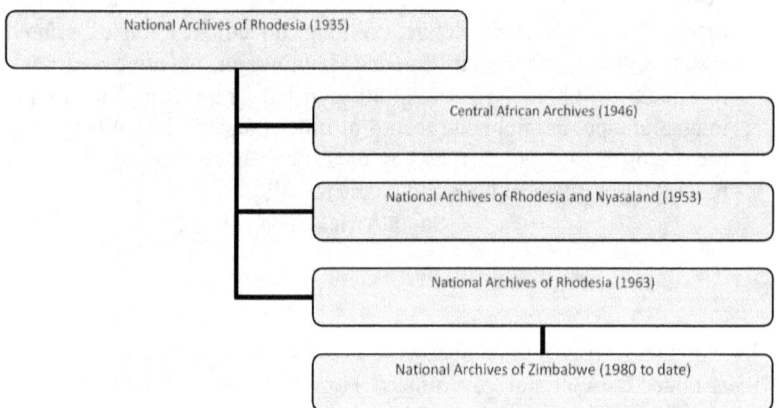

Figure 1.3 Predecessor institutions of the National Archives of Zimbabwe

Long Description: Figure showing archival institutions that preceded the National Archives of Zimbabwe starting from the National Archives of Rhodesia (1935) with relationships with the Central African Archives (1946), National Archives of Rhodesia and Nyasaland (1953), National Archives of Rhodesia (1963) and eventual National Archives of Zimbabwe (from 1980 to date)

Source: (Chaterera, 2016, p. 120)

The National Archives of Zimbabwe Act (Chapter 25:06) provides for the continuity of those archives after the repeal of their creating legislation, "for the storage and preservation of public archives and public records" (Section 3). Public archives are defined as:

(a) Any public record which –
　i　Is twenty-five years old; and
　ii　Has been specified by the Director as being of enduring or historical value; or

(b) Any other record or material acquired for the National Archives by the Director.

(Section 2)

Public records, in turn, are defined solely based on custody: "public record means any record in the custody of any Ministry" (Section 2). Thus, those records that fall within the purview of the National Archives of Zimbabwe include, but are not limited to, public records. In particular, the director "may acquire by purchase, donation, bequest or otherwise any record or other material which in his opinion is or is likely to be of enduring or historical value" (Section 5(c)). Although the director seemingly has broad powers, he "may, in respect of any Ministry . . . inspect and examine [their] records [and/or] give advice or instructions concerning the filing, maintenance and preservation . . . of [those] records" (Section 6). The director is ultimately limited by the discretion of the Minister responsible for said Ministry, whose decision is final. Similarly, in cases where the director of the National Archives is denied access to records by a local authority, his only recourse is to the relevant Minister, who has ultimate authority to grant or deny such access as s/he/they deem(s) fit. The role of the National Archives of Zimbabwe is largely circumscribed to an advisory role.

Understandably, given the colonial history of Zimbabwe, much of the National Archives Act is concerned with the protection of historical records, and the imposition of penalties upon individuals who would take such records. In the context of broader archival practice, however, the National Archives of Zimbabwe Act is both out of date and stingy in its context and guidance. As Mutsagondo and Chaterera (2016) point out, the Act, having been written in 1986, makes no provision for electronic records. The Act defines "record" broadly enough that electronic records are almost certainly within its purview ("any medium in or on which information is recorded" (Section 2)); however, extraordinarily little guidance is given in the Act itself or in secondary legislation as to what is to be done with and to those records and by whom. As Ngoepe and Saurombe (2016, p. 37) put it, "Zimbabwe does not have archival legislation that specifically caters for the creation, use, maintenance and disposal of electronic records, which has resulted in records management practitioners resorting to a hit-or-miss approach when managing electronic records." Mutsagondo and Chaterera's (2016) survey of records managers working under the Act revealed that such critical areas as records transfer, destruction, authenticity, capacity, and appraisal are all negatively impacted by the lack of legal guidance concerning electronic records. The Act also lacks provisions commonly found in archival laws, such as those providing for the legal authenticity of certified copies of records provided by the archives (be they paper or electronic). While the Act is broad and flexible, and, therefore, could be updated through secondary legislation, there has been no attempt to do so thus far.

> The current legal set-up does not guarantee the controlled management of electronic records throughout their lifecycle, and this potentially robs the country of its documentary heritage. In such circumstances, the country may find it difficult to plan for its present and its future.
> (Mutsagondo and Chaterera, 2016, p. 255)

In all four countries, the national archives and their animating law(s) are a product of the broader legal system, the socioeconomic realities within the country, and the technical and political needs that the archival system serves. As challenging as it may prove with the many other demands upon them, ARM professionals should always remain conscientious as to whom their institutions serve, even if the law is neutral on its face as to which citizens' records it will preserve. As Bhebhe and Ngoepe (2021, p. 156) found in the cases of both Zimbabwe and South Africa, even after liberation from colonization, the national archives – like archives worldwide – are largely controlled by elites who "have shaped the national historical narrative into their favour and to the detriment of the minority groups whose stories have been silenced, distorted, manipulated and obliterated in some cases."

Access to information

Access to information (ATI) laws, also known as right to information (RTI) laws or freedom of information (FOI) laws, reflect the general view that access to information is a fundamental human right. Indeed, Article 9 of the African Charter on Human and Peoples' Rights provides that, "1. Every individual shall have the right to receive information. [and] 2. Every individual shall have the right to express and disseminate his opinions within the law" (Organisation of African Unity, 1981). In its "Declaration of Principles on Freedom of Expression and Access to Information in Africa," the African

Commission on Human and Peoples' Rights (2019, p. 3) declares that "The respect, protection and fulfilment of these rights is crucial and indispensable for the free development of the human person, the creation and nurturing of democratic societies and for enabling the exercise of other rights."

Since the 1980s, regional and international organizations have applied both direct and indirect pressure on the tenets of transparency, good governance, and accountability in public sector reform initiatives globally. Other African examples include the Declaration of Principles on Freedom of Expression in Africa (African Commission on Human and Peoples' Rights, 2002), the African Charter on Democracy, Elections, and Good Governance (African Union, 2007), and the Model Law on Access to Information for Africa (African Commission on Human and People's Rights, 2013). These efforts underpinned the passage of ATI legislation or constitutional provisions in a number of countries from the 1990s through the 2010s (Lemieux and Trapnell, 2016, p. 14). There are two trends in the enactment of ATI in Africa. First, some countries have enacted fully-fledged legislation, often accompanied by implementation regulations. These include South Africa and Zimbabwe in 2002, Uganda in 2005, Liberia and Guinea in 2010, Nigeria in 2011, Cote d'Ivoire and Rwanda in 2013, Burkina Faso in 2015, and Kenya, Malawi, Tanzania, and Tunisia in 2016 (Katuu, 2011; Right2Info, 2021). Secondly, some countries only have a constitutional provision. These include Mozambique in 1990, Ghana and Madagascar in 1992, Seychelles in 1993, Ethiopia in 1994, Guinea Bissau in 1996, Senegal in 2001, Angola in 2002, Democratic Republic of Congo in 2006, and Cape Verde in 2010 (Right2Info, 2021).

ATI laws have been embraced worldwide as "part of the overall global trend toward more transparent and open government" (Lemieux and Trapnell, 2016, p. 1). ATI laws are supposed to

> improv[e] the efficiency of the government and increase[e] the transparency of its functioning by:
>
> - Regularly and reliably providing government documents to the public
> - Educating the public on the significance of transparent government [and]
> - Facilitating appropriate and relevant use of information in people's lives.
>
> (Lemieux and Trapnell, 2016, p. 1)

However, "the ATI debate [globally] has been mostly articulated in terms of 'advances' by legislation . . . this juridical approach to ATI has embedded in it an ideological dimension. . . . the common normative view of diffusion of

ATI is based on an acceptance of liberal values, within the broader context of human rights discourse" (Calland and Diallo, 2013, p. 2). This juridical viewpoint is inescapably embedded in Western values, including constitutionalism and an individualistic approach to rights. Furthermore, as can be seen in this study, mere implementation of ATI laws is no guarantee that information will actually be made available. Indeed, in the case of Zimbabwe, the primary ATI law has been used to suppress and control information that is unfavourable to the government. Thus, ATI laws are far from a panacea. Nonetheless, ARM professionals must understand the obligations that such laws impose and their impact on the transparency and accountability functions of records and archives, as well as their potential to positively impact recordkeeping (Shepherd et al., 2011).

Botswana

Unlike the other countries in this study, Botswana does not have legislation providing for access to information or freedom of information. Khumalo et al. (2016, p. 113) state that the closest to a public right of access to government-held information is Section 12 of the Constitution, which states:

> Except with his or her own consent, no person shall be hindered in the enjoyment of his or her freedom of expression, that is to say, freedom to hold opinions without interference, freedom to receive ideas and information without interference, freedom to communicate ideas and information without interference (whether the communication be to the public generally or to any person or class of persons) and freedom from interference with his or her correspondence.
>
> (Constitution of Botswana, 1966, Section 12)

However, as noted by Khumalo et al. (2016, p. 114), this is a "passive provision for access to information" which provides only "freedom to receive information. . . [and not] to seek information from the government." Botswana's legal framework skews heavily in favour of government secrecy; public officers within the National Archives and Records Services must make an oath of declaration of secrecy (Botswana, 1978 Chapter 59:04, ss9). Indeed, Balule and Dambe (2018, p. 431) go so far as to assert that "openness and transparency are alien concepts in Botswana's democracy," noting that public servants who reveal "any information coming to their knowledge or the nature or content of any documented communicated to them either in the course of their duty or by virtue of their employment [are subject to] summary dismissal" (*Id.*). Disclosure requires permission of the Permanent Secretary of the public servant's ministry (*Id.*).

A number of laws in Botswana, including the National Security Act (Chapter 23 of 1986, amended in 2005), the Cybercrime and Computer Related Crimes Act (Chapter 08:06), the Media Practitioners Act (Act 29 of 2008), and the Intelligence and Security Services Act (Chapter 23:02), strongly favour secrecy over openness. Furthermore, the dimensions of the constitutional right to freedom of information have not been defined.

> After half a century since the adoption of the Constitution, it is perhaps surprising that, given the importance of the right of access to information, and the difficulties faced by individuals in accessing State-held information, courts of law in the country have not yet been called upon to make a determination on the ambit of the right of access to information guaranteed in the Constitution.
>
> (Balule and Dambe, 2018)

There seems to be no movement towards increasing access to information through law or policy (Khumalo et al., 2016).

Kenya

Article 35 of the Constitution of Kenya guarantees both access to information and the right to be forgotten, stating:

> (1) Every citizen has the right of access to –
>
>   (a) information held by the State; and
>   (b) information held by another person and required for the exercise or protection of any right or fundamental freedom.
>
> (2) Every person has the right to the correction or deletion of untrue or misleading information that affects the person.
> (3) The State shall publish and publicise any important information affecting the nation.
>
> (Constitution of Kenya, 2010, Article 35)

How those rights are to be exercised and their limits are further defined in relevant legislation, in particular, the *Access to Information Act*. As Abuya (2013, p. 219) notes, however, this right, which is available to Kenyan citizens only, is subject to Article 24 of the Constitution, which provides that the right of ATI can be limited by "to the extent that the limitation is reasonable and justifiable in an open and democratic society based on human dignity, equality and freedom." Magina (2019, p. 87), in a study examining why Kenyans struggle to access information after the passage of the *Access to Information Act*, identifies the limitation of the right to citizens as "[t]he major limitation of the right of access."

The *Access to Information Act* (Act No. 31 of 2016) is meant to fulfil a number of accountability and transparency goals by providing access to records and other forms of information. The definition of "information" given in the act is extensive, including "all records held by a public entity or a private body, regardless of the form in which the information is stored, its source or the date of production" (Section 2). The inclusion of private bodies is particularly notable; ATI laws often focus only on public bodies.

The legislative purpose of the *Access to Information Act* is to:

(a) give effect to the right of access to information by citizens as provided under Article 35 of the Constitution;
(b) provide a framework for public entities and private bodies to proactively disclose information that they hold and to provide information on request in line with the constitutional principles;
(c) provide a framework to facilitate access to information held by private bodies in compliance with any right protected by the Constitution and any other law;
(d) promote routine and systematic information disclosure by public entities and private bodies on constitutional principles relating to accountability, transparency and public participation and access to information;
(e) provide for the protection of persons who disclose information of public interest in good faith; and
(f) provide a framework to facilitate public education on the right to access information under this Act.

(Access to Information Act, 2016, Section 3)

Kenya's *Access to Information Act* is notable as compared to similar legislation in a number of other jurisdictions for its twin focus on providing access to both public entity and private entity information, in such cases where a private entity either "receives public resources and benefits, utilizes public funds, engages in public functions, provides public service as exclusive contracts to exploit natural resources" (Access to Information Act, 2016, Section 2) or

is in possession of information which is of significant public interest due to its relation to the protection of human rights, the environment or public health and safety, or to exposure of corruption or illegal actions or where the release of the information may assist in exercising or protecting any right.

(Access to Information Act, 2016, Section 2)

Kenya's Access to Information Act also provides a far broader right to information than similar legislation in other jurisdictions; under the Act, "every citizen has the right to access to information held by – (a) the State; and (b) another person where that information is required for the exercise or protection of any right or fundamental freedom" (Section 3). However, the use of the word "citizen" in both the Access to Information Act and Article 35 of the Constitution is important; the High Court in High Court of Kenya Petition No. 43 of 2012, *Famy Care Limited vs. Public Procurement Administrative Review Board & Another* (2012) held that the right of access to information embodied in Article 35 of the Constitution is a right only of natural persons who are Kenyan citizens.

Another area in which the Access to Information Act is noticeably broad is in its definition of "personal information." Under the Access to Information Act, "personal information" means information about an identifiable individual, including, but not limited to –

(a) information relating to the race, gender, sex, pregnancy, marital status, national, ethnic or social origin, colour, age, physical, psychological or mental health, well-being, disability, religion, conscience, belief, culture, language and birth of the individual;
(b) information relating to the education or the medical, criminal or employment history of the individual or information relating to financial transactions in which the individual has been involved;
(c) any identifying number, symbol or other particular assigned to the individual;
(d) the fingerprints, blood type, address, telephone or other contact details of the individual;
(e) a person's opinion or views over another person;
(f) correspondence sent by the individual that is implicitly or explicitly of a private or confidential nature or further correspondence that would reveal the contents of the o original correspondence;
(g) any information given in support or in relation to an award or grant proposed to be given to another person;
(h) contact details of an individual.

(Access to Information Act, 2016, 2)

The inclusion of "correspondence," which encompasses not just data, but also records, is a notable departure from freedom of information legislation in other jurisdictions.

In addition to the duty to fulfil information requests, the Access to Information Act imposes several duties upon ARM professions in public entities. Article 17 provides for the "management of records," which are defined as "documents or other sources of information compiled, recorded or stored in written form or in any other manner and includes electronic records." Section 17(2) requires that public entities:

> keep and maintain –
>
> (a) records that are accurate, authentic, have integrity and useable; and
> (b) its records in a manner which facilitates the right of access to information as provided for in this Act.

Section17(3) imposes a duty on public entities to document and a requirement to digitize.

The duty to document requires that public entities, at a minimum, "create and preserve such records as are necessary to document adequately [the entity's] policies, decisions, procedures, transactions and other activities it undertakes pertinent to the implementation of its mandate" (Section 17(3)(a)). The digitization requirement demands that, "not later than three years from the date from which this Act begins to apply to [a public entity, the entity shall] computerize its records and information management systems" (Section 17(3)(c)).

The *County Governments Act* (No. 17 of 2012), imposes access to information obligations upon government at the county level, stating that one of the principles of citizen participation in county government is "timely access to information, data, documents, and other information relevant or related to policy formulation and implementation" (Section 87(a)). Article 96 provides directly for the right of access to information vis-à-vis county government, stating that:

> Every county government and its agencies shall designate an office for purposes of ensuring access to information as required by subsection (1)(3). Subject to national legislation governing access to information, a county government shall enact legislation to ensure access to information.
> (*County Governments Act*, 2012, Art. 96, Sec. 2)

South Africa

Lemieux and Trapnell (2016) characterize South Africa as being in the "middle" range of countries with regard to ATI – those countries that have implemented ATI laws but are still facing challenges. The authors state that: "South Africa has an active human rights commission that conducts regular evaluations and training for civil servants but lacks enforcement authority and faces the challenge of low capacity within the civil service" (Lemieux and Trapnell, 2016, p. 4). South Africa's ATI law is the *Promotion of Access to Information Act* (No. 2 of 2000, hereinafter PAIA). PAIA, which finds its analogue in other jurisdictions' freedom of information legislation, makes meaningful the promise of access to information in Section 32 of the Constitution.

PAIA explicitly overrides all limitations on the disclosure of records in other legislation if those limitations are in conflict with the purposes or a specific provision of PAIA (Section 5). PAIA sets out guidance for accessing information held by two types of bodies: public bodies and private bodies. The statute places authority for PAIA on both the records holders and the South African Human Rights Commission, which receives the mandatory PAIA manuals from various bodies and provides PAIA guidance. PAIA provides procedural guidance on how to access information held by both public and private bodies, addressing issues including the right of access, manner of access, time limits for response, grounds for refusal, and third-party notice and intervention.

PAIA protects information officers who act in good faith, shielding them from any civil or criminal liability from attempting to discharge their duties under PAIA. However, for the individual who acts in bad faith, this law imposes potential criminal liability:

> A person who with intent to deny a right of access in terms of this Act- (a) destroys, damages or alters a record; (b) conceals a record; or (c) falsifies a record or makes a false record, commits an offence and is liable on conviction to a fine or to imprisonment for a period not exceeding two years.
>
> (Section 90(1))

Two major – and, as of the time of writing, unresolved – points of conflict between the National Archives Act and PAIA must be pointed out. The first is a question of responsibility: the National Archives Act gives extensive powers to the National Archives, whereas PAIA centres authority for South Africa's information regime in the Department of Justice and Constitutional Development. The second is a question of records release. The National Archives Act provides that information should be made available automatically after 20 years but gives the National Archivist the authority to make records available sooner. PAIA, by contrast, empowers public bodies to decide, and make known through their manuals, what information is automatically available. These conflicts in the law are not resolved.

Zimbabwe

The Constitution of Zimbabwe Amendment (No. 20 of 2013) guarantees the right of access to information. Section 20 of the Lancaster House Constitution also provides for the "freedom to hold opinions and to receive and impart ideas without interference." Zimbabwe's Access to Information and Protection of Privacy Act (Chapter 10:27) (hereinafter AIPPA) is highly unusual among freedom of information laws. While it provides some of the expected freedom of information provisions, covered in the table law, significant portions of AIPPA are concerned with restrictions on the publication and dissemination of information by media and journalists. AIPPA also applies only to records in the custody or control of public bodies; Zimbabwe currently does not have any controls on data privacy in the private sector beyond common law torts such as invasion of privacy.

Zimbabwe's Access to Information and Protection of Privacy Act functions primarily in support of the state, rather than citizens. Section 80, "Abuse of journalistic privilege," flips the public interest test commonly found in freedom of information legislation on its head. The public interest test typically weighs in favour of releasing information in order to enhance transparency and improve the ability of citizens to hold government accountable. Section 80 of AIPPA, by contrast, provides that publishing "any statement – (i) threatening the interests of defence, public safety, public order, the economic interests of the State, public morality or public health" (Section 80(1)(c)(i)) is an offence, which can be punished with "imprisonment for a period not exceeding two years" (Section 80(1)). In other words, AIPPA requires that information be withheld whenever its publication goes against the interests of the state.

Manganga (2012, p. 104) asserts that, "legislations like Access to Information and Protection of Privacy Act (AIPPA) and the Public Order and Security Act (POSA) have enabled the government to exert a stranglehold over the media, media houses, and the free flow of information since 2002." Moyo (2013, p. 72) states that "The ZANU PF government since 2003 used the draconian AIPPA to shut down five newspapers including the Daily News, an important daily paper harshly critical of the government."

As Calland and Diallo (2013, p. 6) put it, "few scholars or practitioners would be easily convinced that Zimbabwe's 2002 Access to Information and Privacy Act is anything other an ATI law in name alone, given the oppressive use to which it has been put."

ATI and the ARM profession

As can be seen from the previous analysis, while the right to information is important in the realization of other rights and the promotion of good governance, the effectiveness of ATI laws is a product of the realities on the ground. As Adeleke (2013, p. 83) explains, "the judicial right to information is largely irrelevant as a solution to political problems in authoritarian or undemocratic states," a reality demonstrated by the use of AIPPA as a tool of political oppression in Zimbabwe. Even in countries where ATI rights exist as a matter of law, practical barriers often exist to exercising those rights. Abuya (2013, p. 218), writing about ATI in Kenya prior to the implementation of the *Access to Information Act*, sums up a common experience with ATI throughout the studied countries (and indeed, throughout the world): "although the process seems straightforward in theory, several hurdles are faced in reality." The ARM profession is critical to reducing those hurdles – only through good recordkeeping can the necessary information be preserved and made accessible. Indeed, "[m]uch of the argument we advance for the recordkeeping imperative hinges around notions of accountability and audit" ensuring that the accountability of government to its citizens, as provided through ATI, is a central mandate of public records managers (Hofman, 2020, p. 219). Even those in private organizations may find themselves subject to ATI requirements, as noticed previously. However, effective ATI requires more than excellent recordkeeping, regardless of the dedication and efforts of ARM professionals. "ATI is an intricate concept, not easily reduced to simple numbers or laws; it requires complex shifts in power relations and bureaucratic culture for it to take root and flourish" (Calland and Diallo, 2013, p. 8).

Data protection

Privacy and, specifically, balancing privacy and access in the face of digital technologies, have become a universal challenge for ARM professionals. As McLeod (2019, p. 18) writes:

> [f]or cloud users one of the challenges to emerge from the InterPARES research was balancing security, privacy, and access, given their various tensions [including] privacy and access to data and records; between what is public and what is private data; between managing organizational risk in a public accountability context and protecting personal information while still making data public; and balancing democratic goals with those for business innovation.

Botswana

Botswana's *Data Protection Act, 2018* (Act 32 of 2018) has been assented to by Parliament but as of this writing, is not yet in force. The *Data Protection Act* (DPA) is quite modern. As Daigle (2021, p. 14) notes,

> the DPA contains numerous provisions which align with the [European Union's General Data Protection Regulation, the current "gold standard" for data protection], and much of the structure of the law as well as the rights of individuals are very similar to the EU data protection law.

Daigle (2021, p. 14) summarizes some of the major provisions of Botswana's DPA:

> For personal data to be processed legally in Botswana, the consent of the data subject must be gathered (this consent can also be revoked).

In certain circumstances, this consent will not be required – i.e., if data must be processed in order to complete the terms of a contract to which the data subject is a party, to comply with a legal obligation, to protect the data subject's "vital interests," or to perform an activity in the public interest. Data must also be kept for no longer than necessary, and its processing must have a clearly defined purpose. Moreover, firms must ensure that they have taken appropriate security and technical measures to prevent the theft of personal data (though the law does not define what measures specifically must be taken). Fines for noncompliance can reach as high as 500,000 Botswana pula (approximately $43,000) and can include imprisonment for up to nine years.

The potential punishment for violation of the DPA makes it clear that the legislature intended for this law to "have teeth," or to be enforceable.

Kenya

In Kenya, Article 31 of the Constitution provides for a right of privacy; this right, however, is not absolute. Article 24(1) provides for the limitation of fundamental rights in view of countervailing interests. Kenya's *Data Protection Act* (No. 24 of 2019) is very recent, having come into force in 2019, with regulations promulgated in 2020. Like Botswana's *Data Protection Act*, Kenya's DPA aligns fairly closely to the European Union General Data Protection Regulation (EU GDPR), centering the processing of personal data on principles of consent, transparency, and lawfulness, providing data subjects with a number of rights, and imposing duties on data controllers and processors. Of particular note to ARM professionals is Article 53, which provides exemptions for the processing of data for "historical, statistical or research purposes," which will likely include archives. The DPA also established the Office of the Data Protection Commissioner (www.odpc.go.ke/), which is tasked under Article 8 with overseeing the implementation of the Act, establishing and maintaining a register of data controllers and processors, providing oversight on data processing, and investigating and inspecting data processing operations.

Some further statutes also provide grounds for data privacy claims. Article 31 of the *Kenya Information and Communications Act* (No. 1 of 2009) makes it an offence for telecommunications firms to unlawfully intercept messages from their clients or to disclose such messages, while Article 83 of the same Act makes unauthorized access to a computer system an offence. In the *Banking (Credit Reference Bureau) Regulations*, 2013, Article 49 et seq., data protection measures such as processing limitations, purpose specification, and information quality are imposed, but only upon the small sector of credit reporting. Such data protection mechanisms are not required more broadly.

Informational privacy, including privacy in records, is also undermined by the use of data surveillance by the state security apparatus. Kenya has passed a number of laws enabling data surveillance, including the *National Intelligence Service (NIS) Act*, 2012; the *Security Laws (Amendment) Act*, 2014; and the Prevention of Terrorism Act (2012). This pattern is not unique to Kenya – state security is often the justification for both secrecy and surveillance. Under these laws, fundamental rights – such as privacy and access to information – are limited or even suspended in the pursuit of countervailing state interests. These laws include provisions that directly concern ARM professionals. For example, the National Intelligence Service (NIS) Act (2012), in Article 45, empowers

> an officer of the Service . . . to obtain any information, material, record, document or thing and for that purpose – (a) to enter any place, or obtain access to anything; (b) to search for or remove or return, examine, take extracts from, make copies of or record in any other manner the information, material, record document or thing; (c) to monitor communication; or (d) install, maintain or remove anything.

The Security Laws (Amendment) Act (2014) provides explicitly for limiting of the right of privacy, stating that,

> (1) The National Security Organs may intercept communication for the purposes of detecting, deterring and disrupting terrorism in accordance with procedures to be prescribed by the Cabinet Secretary. . . . (3) The right to privacy under Article 31 of the Constitution shall be limited under this section for the purpose of intercepting communication directly relevant in the detecting, deterring and disrupting terrorism.

On the other hand, the security apparatus is also used to deny access to records, including those that are ostensibly public. For example, the Official Secrets Act, Cap. 187 (Act No. 31 of 2016), makes it an offence for anyone who

> obtains, collects, records, publishes or communicates in whatever manner to any other person any code word, plan, article, document or information which is calculated to be or might be or is intended to be directly or indirectly useful to a foreign power or disaffected person.
> (Section 3(1)(c))

South Africa

The *Protection of Personal Information Act* (POPI Act) operationalizes the right to privacy in Section 14 of the Constitution. This sophisticated data protection act, which came into effect in 2020, outlines the rights of data subjects, the obligations, both in terms of rights and security, of data processors, and the mechanisms for enforcement; it applies to the collection, storage, use, dissemination, and deletion of personal information (and thus applies to all recordkeeping and archives that deal with people's individually identifiable information). The statute embodies accepted data protection principles: "The conditions for the lawful processing of personal information by or for a responsible party are the following: [accountability, processing limitation, purpose specification, further processing limitation, information quality, openness, security safeguards, and data subject participation]" (Section 4(1)). Lawful data collection and processing under POPI requires the party responsible for the processing to:

- ensure compliance with the POPI Act;
- not use personal information beyond the purpose for which it was given;
- only process personal information where:
  - the data subject or their surrogate has consented;
  - processing is necessary for a contract to which the data subject is a party;
  - processing complies with an obligation imposed by law on the responsible party;
  - processing protects a legitimate interest of the data subject;
  - processing is necessary for the proper performance of a public law duty by a public body; or
  - processing is necessary for pursuing the legitimate interests of the responsible party or of a third party to whom the information is supplied.
- specify a specific, explicitly defined, and lawful purpose for the collection of personal information.

Of particular concern to ARM professionals is Section 14, "Retention and restriction of records." This section sets out several different retention requirements for records containing personal information:

- Records must be maintained for the minimum time to achieve the purpose for which the information was collected, *unless*
  - the responsible party needs the record for lawful purposes related to its functions or activities;
  - retention is required by a contract between the parties; or
  - the data subject or his/her surrogate consents to longer retention.

- Records may be retained for longer for historical, statistical, or research purposes, as long as there are safeguards to prevent the record being used for other purpose.
- Records *must* be retained when they are used to make a decision about a data subject for a long enough period to give the data subject an opportunity to request access to that record.

Section 14 also requires the responsible part to destroy, delete, or de-identify a record of personal information as soon as possible once the right to retain the record has expired. Pursuant to Section 17, responsible parties must maintain documentation of all processing operations under their responsibility; under Section 19, responsible parties must also secure the integrity and confidentiality of personal information under their control through appropriate security measures. It should also be noted that the regulator may grant exemptions to responsible parties from the requirements of the POPI Act under Sections 37 and 38; Section 37(2)(e) specifically provides for "historical, statistical, or research activity" as a public interest which may justify exemption. The POPI Act also imposes data localization, limiting transborder transfer of personal information to those cases where the receiving jurisdiction has laws providing for the same level of protection as South Africa; the data subject consents to the transfer; the transfer is necessary for the performance of a contract between the data subject and the data processor; the transfer is necessary for the performance of a contract in the interest of the data subject; or the transfer is for the benefit of the data subject and obtaining consent is impracticable, and likely, if it were practicable (Section 72).

However, empirical research has shown a gap between the law's requirements and privacy as practiced in South Africa. Da Veiga (2020, p. 65), reporting on a survey of South Africans, found that "regulatory requirements (in this case, the POPI Act) are perceived as not being met. The results indicate that while consumers in South Africa have a high expectation for privacy, it is not met in practice."

Zimbabwe

Section 57 of the constitution of Zimbabwe guarantees the right of privacy; some of those guarantees are relevant to records in that they address data privacy. The relevant constitutional language states, "Every person has the right to privacy, which includes the right not to have – . . . (d) the privacy of their communications infringed; or (e) their health condition disclosed." As Ncube (2016, p. 105) explains, "There is as yet no reported case law on the interpretation of the new Zimbabwean constitutional provisions. However, as they so closely mirror

South African provisions, it is likely that Zimbabwean courts will be persuaded by South African case law." Van der Bank (2012, p. 79), writing on a South African case covering the privacy provisions of the South African Constitution (*S v Nkabinde* 1998 8 BCLR 996 [N]), writes that, "The entrenchment of the right to privacy in [the Constitution] compels the Government to initiate steps to protect neglected aspects of the right to privacy in South Africa, such as data privacy or the protection of personal information." If, then, the Zimbabwean courts interpret South African cases such as *Nkabinde* as persuasive authority, they might well find that similar provisions in the Zimbabwean constitution also compel the government to protect the right privacy. At this point in time, however, the question remains open. At the time of this writing, Zimbabwe has a cybersecurity and data protection bill that has passed the Senate and is awaiting presidential approval. However, the proffered data protection bill is deeply problematic.

The *Cyber Security and Data Protection Bill*, 2019, has drawn deep criticism, with Transparency International arguing that the bill "will obstruct the crucial role of civil society and the media in the fight against corruption and undermine any recent progress." One section that critics point to is 164B, "Cyber-bullying and harassment." Section 164B provides that

> any person who unlawfully and intentionally by means of a computer or information system generates and sends any data message . . . with the intent to . . . degrade, humiliate or demean the person of another . . . shall be guilty of an offence and liable to a fine not exceeding level 10 or to imprisonment for a period not to exceed ten years.
>
> Transparency International (2020)

Critics read this section – not unreasonably – as threatening up to ten years prison for people who use the Internet to criticize political figures. The "data protection" bill does include many of the EU GDPR provisions seen in other data protection bills, such as duties of data controllers and processors. But, by wedding data privacy to cyber security and, particularly, to a cyber-security bill with extensive focus on criminal pity, the *Cyber Security and Data Protection Bill* makes it clear that privacy does not extend to the state's surveillance apparatus. Ncube (2016, p. 99) is quite frank in describing the state of data privacy in Zimbabwe:

> [The] perceived and experienced vulnerability [of people's personal data] is exacerbated by the fact that there is a general lack of knowledge about existing legal protection of privacy. The legislative framework does little to assuage this vulnerability because it is currently inadequate.

Makulilo (2016, p. 372), considering the data privacy regimes in a number of African countries comparatively, states, "Zimbabwe [is] characterised [among the] authoritarian states. The surveillance context in each of the countries in Africa partly reflects its democratic status."

Data protection and data colonialism

Finally, ARM professionals should maintain an awareness that data has become a resource, specifically, a resource that Western technological firms are trying to extract and exploit. Data protection laws are often posited as a solution to this problem but are even more inadequate to protect Africans' data privacy than they are to protect Americans' data privacy. According to Coleman (2019, p. 423), "[u]nder digital colonialism, foreign powers, led by the United States, are planting infrastructure in the Global South engineered for [their] own needs, enabling economic and cultur[al] domination while imposing privatized forms of governance." In other words, because there is so much economic value to be extracted by establishing a virtual monopoly in order to take Africans' personal data for advertising and predictive analytics, American companies like Facebook and Alphabet (the parent company of Google) are strongly incentivized to build (subpar) infrastructure – "poor internet for poor people" – in order to deliver those peoples' data to the companies (Biddle, 2017). While such companies have been vacuuming up Westerners' personal data for years now, the situations are not the same. In countries such as the United State, extensive Internet infrastructure is already in place, which allows greater access without being held captive by an entity such as Facebook.

Furthermore, "big tech companies can violate (and have blatantly violated) [data protection] laws, since they have the time, money, and resources to fight for their desired outcomes, even if they stand in direct violation of pre-established law" (Coleman, 2019, p. 433). Indeed, penalties and fines are simply a cost of doing business, and are far lower than the value that Facebook or Alphabet extracts from its illegal conduct. Even if the law could provide for consequences that would have a deterrent impact – as, arguably, Kenya's Data Protection Law could by – there is not guarantee of meaningful impacts. As Coleman argued prior to the Data Protection Law's passage: "[l]arge tech companies and data brokers could simply dissolve before they ever have to face any accountability measures" (Coleman, 2019, p. 435).

ARM professionals, then, are in the delicate position of having to ensure their compliance with data protection regulations while ensuring the trustworthiness of their records, and doing so in a way that takes advantage of all available resources without imposing undue risk. This challenge is amplified by data protection bills that are anything but, and digital colonists offering cheap "solutions" that impose new kinds of privacy problems.

Conclusion

ARM professionals must balance a number of competing requirements, values, and priorities, often in under-resourced environments, and in the face of sometimes incredible legal complexity. In Botswana, Kenya, South Africa, and Zimbabwe, they must balance the recordkeeping requirements of archives-specific laws with the transparency-needs from ATI-laws and the protection of data subjects' privacy and data. Furthermore, the letter of the law may well depart from the reality on the ground, like when an "access to information" law is used to limit the media and control dissent. Finally, ARM professionals in the countries in this study, operating as they do in post-colonial societies that are still navigating the fallout of colonization on both their legal and bureaucratic systems, must remain continuously aware of the power dynamics inherent in recordkeeping, and the values they and their institutions serve, and should serve. These professionals carry the heavy burden of meeting the requirements of the law while serving the needs of their whole community, including those whose voices are silenced, towards a better future. As Bhebhe and Ngoepe (2021, p. 155) remind us, "those who are oppressed would always find a way of expressing themselves and try to shape the world they want to live." ARM professionals must listen carefully for those expressions.

Notes

1 A table of laws and references examined is available on the InterPARES Trust website.
2 This is not, however, a universal view: "Eduard Fagan . . . says that there has been much support, both judicial and academic, for the view that South African law is a legal system in its own right" (Fombad, 2010, p. 6).

References

Abuya, E. (2013). 'Realizing the right of access to information in Kenya: What should stakeholders be on the lookout for?' in F. Diallo and R. Calland (eds.). *Access to information in Africa: Law, culture and practice.* Lieden: Brill, pp. 215–244.

Adeleke, F. (2013). 'Constitutional domestication of the right of access to information in Africa: Retrospect and prospects,' in F. Diallo and R. Calland (eds.). *Access to information in Africa: Law, culture and practice.* Leiden, Netherlands: Brill, pp. 83–105.

African Commission on Human and Peoples' Rights. (2002). *Declaration of principles on freedom of expression in Africa.* Available at: www.right2info.org/resources/publications/instruments-and-standards/africa_declaration-of-principles-on-freedom-of-expression-in-africa (Accessed 8 August 2021).

African Commission on Human and People's Rights. (2013). *Model law on access to information for Africa*. Available at: www.achpr.org/files/news/2013/04/d84/model_law.pdf (Accessed 7 December 2017).

African Commission on Human and Peoples' Rights. (2019). *Declaration of principles on freedom of expression and access to information in Africa*. Available at: www.achpr.org/public/Document/file/English/draft_declaration_of_principles_on_freedom_of_expression_in_africa_eng.pdf (Accessed 8 August 2021).

African Union. (2007). *African charter on democracy, elections and good governance*. Available at: www.right2info.org/resources/publications/instruments-and-standards/africa_charter-on-dem-elections-and-gov_2007_eng (Accessed 8 August 20210.

Balule, T. B. and B. J. Dambe. (2018). 'The right of access to state-held information in Botswana: Lessons from emerging international human rights jurisprudence,' *Commonwealth Law Bulletin*, 44 (3), pp. 429–451.

Bhebhe, S. and Ngoepe, M. (2021). 'Elitism in critical emancipatory paradigm: National archival oral history collection in Zimbabwe and South Africa,' *Archival Science*, 21, pp. 155–172.

Biddle, E. R. (2017). *The more we connect, the better it gets – for Facebook*. Available at: www.nytimes.com/2017/09/26/opinion/facebook-free-basics.html (Accessed 24 September 2021).

Botswana. (1978). *National archives and records services cap 59*. Available at: https://botswanalaws.com/alphabetical-list-of-statutes/national-archives-and-records-services (Accessed 20 July 2021).

Botswana. (2014a). *Electronic communications and transactions act 14 of 2014*. Available at: https://botswanalaws.com/alphabetical-list-of-statutes/electronic-communications-and-transactions (Accessed 20 July 2021).

Botswana. (2014b). *Electronic records (evidence) act 13 of 2014*. Available at: https://botswanalaws.com/alphabetical-list-of-statutes/electronic-records-evidence (Accessed 20 July 2021).

Calland, R. and Diallo, F. (2013). 'Introduction: Navigating the transparency landscape in Africa,' in F. Diallo and R. Calland (eds.). *Access to information in Africa: Law, culture and practice*. Lieden: Brill, pp. 1–9.

Chaterera, F. (2016). 'Managing public records in Zimbabwe: The road to good governance, accountability, transparency and effective service delivery,' *Journal of the South African Society of Archivists*, 49, pp. 116–136.

Chesworth, J. A. (2010). 'Islamic courts in Kenya and Tanzania: Reactions and responses,' The Centre for Muslim-Christian Studies Newsletter. Available at: www.cmcsoxford.org.uk/s/Chesworth-Islamic-Courts-in-Kenya-and-Tanzania-CMCS-News-10-02.pdf (Accessed 9 October 2021).

Clegg, M., Ellena, K. et al. (2016). *The hierarchy of laws understanding and implementing the legal frameworks that govern elections*. Arlington, VA: International Foundation for Electoral Systems.

Coleman, D. (2019). 'Digital colonialism: The 21st century scramble for Africa through the extraction and control of user data and the limitations of data protection laws,' *Michigan Journal of Race and Law*, 24 (2), pp. 417–439.

Cornell Law School. (2020). *Legal systems*. Available at: www.law.cornell.edu/wex/legal_systems (Accessed 23 September 2021).

Daigle, B. (2021). 'Data protection laws in Africa: A pan-African survey and noted trends,' *Journal of International Commerce and Economics*, pp. 1–27.

Darch, C. (2013). 'The problem of access to information in african jurisdictions: Constitutionalism, citizenship, and human rights discourse,' in F. Diallo and R. Calland (eds.). *Access to information in Africa: Law, culture and practice*. Leiden, Netherlands: Brill, pp. 27–53.

Da Veiga, A. (2020). 'Concern for information privacy in South Africa: An empirical study using the OIPCI,' *Information and Cyber Security 19th International Conference*, Pretoria, South Africa, Springer.

Diala, A. C. and Kangwa, B. (2019). 'Rethinking the interface between customary law and constitutionalism in sub-Saharan Africa,' *De Jure Law Journal*, 52 (1), pp. 189–206.

Fombad, C. (2010). 'Mixed systems in Southern Africa: Divergences and convergences,' *Tulane European and Civil Law Forum*, 25 (1), pp. 1–22.

Garner, B. A. (1995). *A dictionary of modern legal usage*. New York: Oxford University Press.

Georgiadis, K. M. (2012). *The emerging jurisprudence on the right of access to information in Kenya*. Available at: https://ssrn.com/abstract=2257151 (Accessed 23 September 2021).

Hofman, D. (2020). *Between knowing and not knowing: Privacy, transparency and digital records*. University of British Columbia, Vancouver. PhD thesis.

Katuu, S. (2011). 'Freedom of information in Africa,' in *Strengthening governance in the electronic environment: Managing records as reliable evidence for ICT/e-government and freedom of information*. Available at: www.researchgate.net/publication/322301296_Freedom_of_Information_in_Africa (Accessed 24 September 2021).

Katuu, S. (2020). 'Exploring the challenges facing archives and records professionals in Africa: Historical influences, current developments and opportunities,' in R. Edmondson, L. Jordan and A. C. Prodan (eds.). *The UNESCO memory of the world programme: Key aspects and recent developments*. Cham, Switzerland: Springer Nature, pp. 275–292.

Katuu, S. and Ngoepe, M. (2015). 'Managing digital records within South Africa's legislative and regulatory framework,' *3rd International Conference on Cloud Security and Management ICCSM-2015*. B. E. Popovsky. Tacoma, WA, USA, University of Washington – Tacoma, pp. 59–70.

Kenya Judiciary. (2021). *Structure of courts*. Available at: www.judiciary.go.ke/courts/ (Accessed 23 September 2021).

Khan, N. (2020). 'Custom, culture and law in colonial, anti-colonial and postcolonial times,' *Birkbeck Law Review*, 7 (1), pp. 1–25.

Khumalo, N. B., Mosweu, O., et al. (2016). 'A comparative study of freedom of information legislation in Botswana, South Africa and Zimbabwe,' *Mousaion*, 34 (4), pp. 108–131.

Lemieux, V. L. and Trapnell, S. E. (2016). *Public access to information for development: A guide to the effective implementation of right to information laws*. Washington DC: World Bank Publications.

Magina, A. (2019). *Access to information in Kenya: A critical analysis of the access to information act 2016*. University of Nairobi, Nairobi. Master's thesis.

Makulilo, A. B. (2016). 'The future of data protection in Africa,' in A. B. Makulilo (ed.). *African data privacy laws*. Cham: Springer, 33, pp. 371–379.

Malila, I. S. (2010). 'Reconciling plural legal systems: Between justice and social disorder in Botswana,' *Botswana Notes and Records*, 42, pp. 71–78.

Manganga, K. (2012). 'The internet as public sphere: A Zimbabwean case study (1999–2008),' *Africa Development*, 37 (1), pp. 103–118.

McLeod, J. (2019). 'The cloud: Challenges and issues,' in L. Duranti and C. Rogers (eds.). *Trusting records in the cloud: The creation, management, and preservation of trustworthy digital content*. London, UK: Facet Publishing, pp. 13–36.

Mosweu, T. and Simon, I. (2018). 'The implications of the national archives and records services act on archival practice in Botswana,' *Journal of the South African Society of Archivists*, 51, pp. 70–96.

Moyo, S. (2013). 'Regime survival strategies in Zimbabwe in the 21st century,' *African Journal of Political Science and International Relations*, 7 (2), pp. 67–78.

Mutsagondo, S. and F. Chaterera. (2016). 'Mirroring the National Archives of Zimbabwe Act in the context of electronic records lessons for ESARBICA member states,' *Information Development*, 32 (3), pp. 254–259.

Ncube, C. B. (2016). *Data protection in Zimbabwe. African Data Privacy Laws*. A. B. Makulilo. Cham: Springer, 33, pp. 99–116.

Ngoepe, M. and Saurombe, A. (2016). 'Provisions for managing and preserving records created in networked environments in the archival legislative frameworks of selected member states of the Southern African Development Community,' *Archives and Manuscripts*, 44 (1), pp. 24–41.

Organisation of African Unity. (1981). *African charter on human and peoples' rights*. Available at: https://au.int/sites/default/files/treaties/36390-treaty-0011_african_charter_on_human_and_peoples_rights_e.pdf (Accessed 20 July 2021).

Osiro, R. (2013). 'Women's views on the role of Kadhi's courts: A case study of Kendu Bay, Kenya,' in J. Chesworth and F. Kogelmann (eds.). *Sharī'a in Africa today: Reactions and responses*. Leiden: Brill, pp. 149–176.

Palmer, V. V. (2012). 'Mixed legal systems,' in M. Bussani and U. Mattei (eds.). *The Cambridge companion to comparative law*. Cambridge: Cambridge University Press, pp. 368–383.

Republic of Kenya (2010). *Kenya constitution*. Available at: www.kenyalaw.org:8181/exist/kenyalex/actview.xql?actid=Const2010 (Accessed 21 July 2021

Right2Info. (2021). *Constitutional provisions, laws and regulations*. Available at: www.right2info.org/laws/constitutional-provisions-laws-and-regulations (Accessed 8 August 2021).

Shepherd, E., Stevenson, A., et al. (2011). 'Records management in English local government: The effect of freedom of information,' *Records Management Journal*, 21 (2), pp. 122–134.

South Africa. (1996). *National archives act 43 of 1996*. Available at: www.info.gov.za/gazette/acts/1996/a43-96.htm (Accessed 20 July 2021).

Van der Bank, C. M. (2012). 'The right to privacy – South African and comparative perspectives,' *European Journal of Business and Social Sciences*, 1 (6), pp. 77–86.

Van der Merwe, C. (2012). 'The origin and characteristics of the mixed legal systems of South Africa and Scotland and their importance in globalisation,' *Fundamina: A Journal of Legal History*, 18 (1), pp. 91–114.

Wallis, M. (2019). 'Interpretation before and after *Natal Joint Municipal Pension Fund v Endument Municipality* 2012 (4) SA 593 (SCA),' *Potchefstroomse Elektroniese Regsblad/Potchefstroom Electronic Law Journal*, 22 (1), pp. 1–29.

Wario, H. A. (2013). 'Debates on Kadhi's courts and Christian-Muslim relations in Isiolo Town: Thematic issues and emergent trends,' in J. Chesworth and F. Kogelmann (eds.). *Sharī'a in Africa today: Reactions and responses*. Leiden: Brill, pp. 149–176.

2 Digital records infrastructure in Botswana, Kenya, South Africa, and Zimbabwe

Forget Chaterera-Zambuko, Mehluli Masuku, and Sindiso Bhebhe

Introduction

Digital infrastructure facilitates the implementation of a variety of digital economy components, including enterprise content management (ECM), enterprise resource planning (ERP), cloud computing, and others. Such digital infrastructure is required to meet the new demands for virtual services in a timely and cost-effective manner (Walwyn and Cloete, 2020). In this chapter, cloud computing, ECM systems, and ERP systems are examples of digital records infrastructure that organizations can use to manage their digital assets or records. ECM and enterprise-wide systems are concerned with the use of comprehensive and all-encompassing strategies, tools, implementation, procedures, and capabilities for the management of all information assets in the form of structured and unstructured data. This includes information management in all media, locations, states of use, and transmissions, which may include digital assets, data in a cloud environment, web content, metadata, and transitory information. ECM systems that work effectively aid in the controlled capture, management, storage, preservation, and accurate referral of information and digital assets. As a result, ECM systems can benefit record management by providing security, accuracy, efficiency, authority, accountability, and transparency. An ERP system is defined as "an integrated information technology (IT) system that uses common databases and consistent cross-functional information flow to allow organizations to integrate information from different departments and locations" (Tsai et al., 2012, P. 36). The overall concept of an ERP system is that business modules generating and capturing information relating to various business activities/sections such as sales, marketing, manufacturing, distribution, personnel, and finance can be supported by a single integrated system with all of the company's data captured in a central database (Holland et al., 1999).

In Botswana, Kenya, South Africa, and Zimbabwe, there is a visible effort to address digital records infrastructure issues. The following sections provide an overview of research conducted in the countries under consideration in this chapter. Despite these studies, implementations of ECM, ERP, and cloud computing systems have been poorly documented. The four countries represented in this chapter have complex political, social, economic, and technological histories that, when combined, contribute to the development and climate of digital assets and records stored in networked environments.

For example, in Zimbabwe, the public sector, which influences the current climate for the presence and development of digital infrastructure, still faces numerous challenges. Zimbabwe's economy remains unstable, perpetuating infrastructure and regulatory deficiencies. Economic uncertainty and high external debt burdens had devastating effects on the development of legislation and policy, human resources, physical infrastructure, health care, and education and training, making future development and planning difficult. These deficiencies have hampered the implementation of several initiatives, including the use of ECM systems, ERP systems, and cloud computing to manage digital assets and records.

A substantial financial investment is required to acquire the necessary application products and to capacitate the people who will be working with the systems. In a country beset by instabilities, records management is one of the areas most harmed by a lack of resources. Nengomasha and Chikomba (2018, p. 254) argue that there were no prescribed methods or steps to be followed when implementing an electronic document record management system (EDRMS), which is one of the tools in the ECM toolbox. This was due to the fact that there was no single office in charge of spearheading, controlling, or monitoring the implementation of EDRMSs. Individual public sector organizations, such as the Central Computing Services (CCS) and the Office of the President and Cabinet (OPC), implemented the system as they saw fit. As a result, determining which public sector organizations in Zimbabwe had actually implemented EDRMSs was difficult. By 2018, the majority of Zimbabwe's public sector organizations had not implemented EDRMSs (Nengomasha and Chikomba, 2018, p. 258). The situation was still the same in 2022.

According to the permanent secretary of the Ministry of Information, Communication Technology, and Courier Services, efforts to implement the system in more organizations have met with resistance, most likely due to "fear of change." People were afraid of migrating to a digital environment because they were used to keeping paper records. In response to this scenario, the National Archives of Zimbabwe prepared a digital transition framework (DTF), which was in the process of being reviewed by stakeholders at the time the study was conducted. The framework was also designed to help organizations manage change as they implement EDRMSs.

On the other hand, South Africa has made significant progress in improving its digital infrastructure. The most recent development is its 2021 Draft National Policy on Data and Cloud. The overarching objective of the draft is to "create an enabling environment for the provision of data and cloud services to ensure socioeconomic development for inclusivity" (Department of Communications and Digital Technologies, 2021). The draft policy has six key objectives, but of particular interest in terms of digital infrastructure is the one that seeks to "promote connectivity and access to data and cloud services," and the one that seeks to "ensure the implementation of effective cyber security, privacy, and data cloud infrastructure protection measures" as reported by the Department of Communications and Digital Technologies (2021). If implemented successfully, this policy has the potential to propel South Africa's digital infrastructure, allowing the country to make up for lost digital opportunities that, according to Walwyn and Cloete (2020), saw South Africa fall to position 104 out of 144 countries in the International Telecommunications Union's Information Society Index of (2018). The index measures countries' progress towards becoming information societies using readiness, intensity, and skills (Walwyn and Cloete, 2020).

Shibambu and Ngoepe (2020) argue that, while public servants save some records informally and unconsciously in the cloud, government departments in South Africa are hesitant to entrust their records to the cloud due to a lack of trust in cloud storage, jurisdiction, legal implications, privacy and security risks associated with the Minimum Information Security Standards, and a lack of policy and legislative framework regarding cloud storage. Because of the lack of infrastructure for management and preservation of digital records, for the purpose of increased storage and access, Shibambu and Ngoepe (2020, p. 1) recommend that "government departments should cautiously consider exploring the possibility of storing their records in a trusted digital repository cloud as an interim solution."

Despite the advent of cloud computing, the South African government is still grappling with manual, paper-based records challenges because no government-owned cloud has been developed to manage and dispose of records (Shibambu and Marutha, 2021). According to Ngoepe (2017, p. 41), "the South African government should also consider creating its private cloud for the management of public records." It is worth noting that the South African government has enacted a policy on free and open-source software, despite the fact that adoption is low (Ngoepe, 2015). South Africa has a long history of implementing ECM, with organizations such as Rand Water, a utility company, implementing its first system equivalent to an ECM system in 1991 (Ngoepe, 2017). South Africa went so far as to evaluate a number of ECM solutions to establish a panel of products for digital records management. The panel's purpose was to allow public entities to shorten tender processes by procuring from the panel through a request for quotation, which is a much shorter process than other tender processes.

The situation in Kenya is different. Despite the fact that organizations in Kenya have begun to use cloud computing services, ResearchICTafrica.net (2017) reports that the government has provided little support to the cloud industry. This is also emphasized by Mosweu et al. (2019, p. 5) that despite the government's ability to ignite the industry through policy support and pledges to cloud services, the information and communication technology (ICT) authority in charge of ICT services has issued a cloud service standard that is not being enforced. Procurement laws are also outdated and continue to reflect traditional methods of procuring ICT hardware and services (ResearchICTafrica.net, 2017).

Kenya also pronounced its Digital Economy Blueprint, which outlines five pillars of a digital economy: digital government, digital business, infrastructure, innovation-driven entrepreneurship, and digital skills and values. The Blueprint's infrastructure domain has a key deliverable, "the availability of affordable, accessible, resilient, and reliable infrastructure" (Republic of Kenya, 2019). Through this key objective, the Kenyan government commits to providing physical and digital infrastructure to connect every Kenyan, commercial entity, and government or public facility, including hospitals, schools, post offices, police stations, and prisons (Republic of Kenya, 2019). According to the Republic of Kenya, this infrastructure has four key deliverables: connectivity and devices, data governance, logistics, and energy, with each deliverable under the objective having specific indicators (2019). This is a huge step forward in terms of putting the digital framework into action.

Botswana has seen the growth of cloud technologies within its borders, where businesses have embraced the new technology to mobilize and push their operational agenda with the same tenacity as the rest of the world by using the technology (Khanda and Doss, 2018, p. 468). Cloud computing has taken root in Botswana, indicating that many small and medium-sized enterprises (SMEs) are using the technology, while others are not. However, as noted by Moatlhodi (2015), the lack of capacity for records management staff to manage records in an electronic environment was an impediment to the implementation of the National Archives and Records Management System (NARMS) in Botswana's then Ministry of Labour and Home Affairs.

ECM implementation can help to advance e-government initiatives by reducing reliance on paper and enabling records to be shared, circulated, and signed online. A government department can capture and store documents digitally using a standard ECM implementation, while allowing users to edit documents based on access rights. ECM systems facilitate information sharing among government agencies in addition to promoting e-government initiatives. Using ECM systems, government officials can retrieve documents remotely using full-text search, and documents can be routed automatically to the right people at the right time. Sharing information between ministries can help with risk management, policymaking, and statistical analysis, among other government activities. As a result, services have improved, as have transparency and accountability. To ensure that proper records and information management principles are embedded in such systems, an organization's leadership responsible for the administration of ECM systems and ERP systems must establish close ties with the records and information department right from the stage of conceptualizing or selecting such systems. Thus, records management should not be an afterthought, but should be deliberately integrated into systems prior to their implementation.

Placing digital records infrastructure into perspective: ECM systems, ERP systems, and cloud computing

Digital infrastructure refers to tools, facilities, applications, systems, platforms, devices, and even strategies that support the use of both existing and emerging technologies. Similarly, in records management, digital records infrastructure refers to products that enable effective management of digital assets and records stored in networked environments. ECM systems, ERP systems, and cloud computing are all examples of digital records infrastructure. It is critical to note that ECM systems are distinct from electronic records management systems (ERMSs) and electronic document management systems (EDMSs) in that ECM systems are the overarching framework with which many components interact, potentially encompassing an ERMS and an EDMS (Katuu, 2012). ECM systems provide an overall framework by integrating multiple systems and procedures to encourage information management throughout its entire life cycle and continuum; thus, they are dependent on a variety of factors and considerations. ECM systems are made up of ten fundamental components, but not all the components are necessarily evident simultaneously. These components or modules include document management, records management, workflow or business process management, collaboration, portals, knowledge management, imaging, digital asset management, digital rights management, and content management (Katuu, 2012, p. 40). Thus, there is a potentially linear or evolutionary relationship between records management and ECM, "with a tendency toward integrated systems oriented toward content management in the digital environment" (Katuu, 2020, p. 46). This means that the ECM framework extends beyond records management and aims to manage information content in all forms using an integrated approach.

In the wake of inevitable changes in several business operations as organizations respond to changing operational needs, transactional systems have emerged as a choice for many institutions as they provide many benefits if implemented correctly. Several institutions have implemented transactional systems such as ERP tools to manage different aspects of their workflows and organizational functions. In this respect, we deemed it prudent to also focus on ERP implementation. Transactional systems such as ERP systems are business applications that integrate the management of core business processes. The areas that can be covered by ERP include accounting, corporate services, customer relationship, data services, human resources, inventorying, workflow management, marketing and sales, order processing, project management, and supply chain management. As such, researchers from Zimbabwe, Kenya, Botswana, and South Africa sought to establish the functional areas that are covered by the transactional system in different institutions that participated in the survey. The researchers were also interested in finding out which companies supply ERP systems in the surveyed institutions.

Many organizations around the world are increasingly utilizing cloud computing, which is Internet-based computing that provides shared computers and other devices on demand. To that end, the study sought to determine whether the institutions that took part in the study used cloud computing to manage their information assets, as well as to comprehend the various reasons for using cloud computing. Cloud computing is a common example of digital records infrastructure that can be used for a variety of purposes, including driving business process transformation, improving security, increasing collaboration, increasing organizational performance, increasing system performance, increasing storage capacity, keeping up with the industry, and lowering costs. There are several cloud computing service models, which are community cloud, hybrid cloud, public cloud, private cloud, a combination of two service models, a combination of three service models, and a combination of four service models. Each cloud has its own set of perceived benefits and drawbacks. The community cloud is known for being compatible among users and convenient since it is easy to control. Community clouds, on the other hand, typically raise security concerns because data is housed in the same location and may be accessed by others who were not intended to access it. Hybrid cloud computing combines private cloud infrastructure with public cloud services. Its main advantage is that it allows for cloud migration. It has more processing power to handle complex workloads, and data is securely protected, though this is debatable. Public clouds are widely used in many organizations, owing to their lower costs and high reliability, whereas private clouds are typically preferred because they are more flexible, provide more control, and provide greater scalability. Overall, no single type of cloud computing can be considered the best. To meet the ongoing and changing needs of organizational functions, organizations typically adopt various cloud computing models.

Regional comparative context

The four countries covered in this chapter are all part of the Eastern and Southern Regional Branch of the International Council on Archives (ESARBICA) region. Despite the fact that countries in the ESARBICA region face similar working conditions and regulatory environments, each is distinct, as explained in Chapter 1 of this book. The ESARBICA region comprises 12 countries: South Africa, Lesotho, Botswana, Namibia, Kenya, Malawi, Mozambique, Swaziland, Tanzania, Zambia, Zimbabwe, and Zanzibar. ESARBICA is a regional branch of the International Council of Archives (ICA), whose aim is to advance collaboration and cooperation in the Eastern and Southern Africa regions. Countries in the ESARBICA region have embraced technological advancements and are all promoting e-government initiatives. The COVID-19 pandemic has pushed governments to become more aggressive in adopting various technologies to offer their services online in an effort to promote social distancing among citizens and, as a result, curb the virus's spread. Although such efforts are commendable, the desired results have only been partially realized due to a lack of adequate knowledge about ECM implementation. Ngoepe (2015, p. 198) mentions some of the challenges, such as contractual obligations with existing vendors that must be honoured and the fact that proprietary ECM is easier to find technical support for than open-source ECM, which takes a long time to fix.

Digital records are becoming more common in the public sector, with increased interest in technological infrastructure, e-government strategies and services, and ICTs. Several studies on electronic records management have been conducted in Botswana, Kenya, South Africa, and Zimbabwe as a result of this growing interest. These studies included, but are not limited to, Sigauke and Nengomasha (2012), Mosweu (2018), Mosweu and Ngoepe (2021), and Maseh (2015). Despite a plethora of studies on electronic records management, the implementation of ECM systems for records management remains limited and isolated.

Data collection and analysis procedures

The SurveyMonkey tool was used to conduct an online survey of the four countries. A closed-ended questionnaire with ten questions was administered, yielding quantitative data. Respondents were required to choose from a list of given options in all questions, implying that there was no room for them to provide their own explanations. This could have been one of the study methodology's shortcomings, as there was no opportunity for respondents to shed more light on the current state of ERP, ECM, and cloud computing services in their organizations. Each question inspired a different theme for data analysis, presentation, and interpretation. Data from all four countries were presented together for each theme/question, resulting in ten thematic areas of data analysis, presentation, analysis, and interpretation. The section that follows is dedicated to the analysis and presentation of primary data gathered through the SurveyMonkey tool, which was used in the four country cases.

ERP and ECM deployment by sector

As a way of facilitating a better understanding of sectoral deployment of ERP and ECM systems, the first question sought to categorize the deployment of the previously described systems by sector (see Figure 2.1).

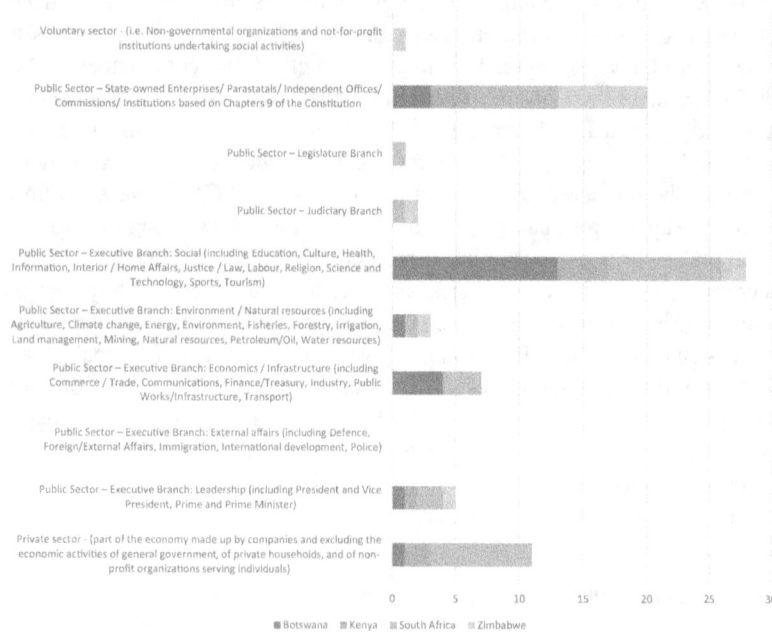

Figure 2.1 ERP and ECM deployment by sector

Long description: Figure 2.1 shows that the deployment of ERP and ECM platforms was dominant in certain sectors. The executive branch (social) was the most dominant in Botswana, followed by state-owned enterprises, and the voluntary sector was last.

Figure 2.1 shows that the deployment of ERP and ECM platforms was dominant in certain sectors. The executive branch (social) was the most dominant in Botswana, followed by state-owned enterprises, and the voluntary sector was last. The 2017 survey yielded similar results in Botswana. In South Africa, the executive branch (social), state-owned enterprises, and the private sector led, while the legislature and the judiciary trailed. The results differ slightly from the 2017 survey in that the executive branch (social) came in first, followed by parastatals and the private sector. The legislature, the executive branch environment, and the executive economics branch received the fewest responses, all of which were equal. Notably, South Africa's private sector emerged as a strong contender in the implementation and use of digital infrastructure in comparison with the same sector in the other three countries. This was also the case in the 2017 survey. In Kenya, a similar situation was reigning, except for the fact that the executive branch (leadership) came last. The current results from Kenya are different from the 2017 results, as the legislature branch recorded the least responses. In the case of Zimbabwe, the picture was slightly different, with parastatals taking the lead, followed by the executive branch (social), while the executive branch (leadership) came last. Different results were obtained in 2017, as the executive branch (social) took the lead, followed by parastatals and the executive branch (leadership). Zimbabwe was the only country in which the voluntary sector registered the deployment of digital infrastructure, albeit to an insignificant extent. It could be of interest to note that the executive branch (external affairs) registered zero presence of digital infrastructure in all four countries. The revelation that the public sector seems to have dominated regarding ERP and ECM systems could be attributed to an observation by Fernandez et al. (2017) that since the early 1980s, governments across the globe have been experimenting with various government reforms. It is such reforms that have seen public sector organizations take the lead in implementing ICTs in an endeavour to improve service delivery.

Scope

Since ERP and ECM are typically deployed on a national, regional, or other localized scale, this question sought to understand the scale on which the aforementioned systems were implemented. According to Uri et al. (2018), ERP enables organizations of any size to support and coordinate their business processes by leveraging virtualization.

In terms of scope as reflected in Figure 2.2, all four countries reported the deployment of ERP and ECM systems in organizations that operated at two levels, namely those that operated on a national scale and those that operated

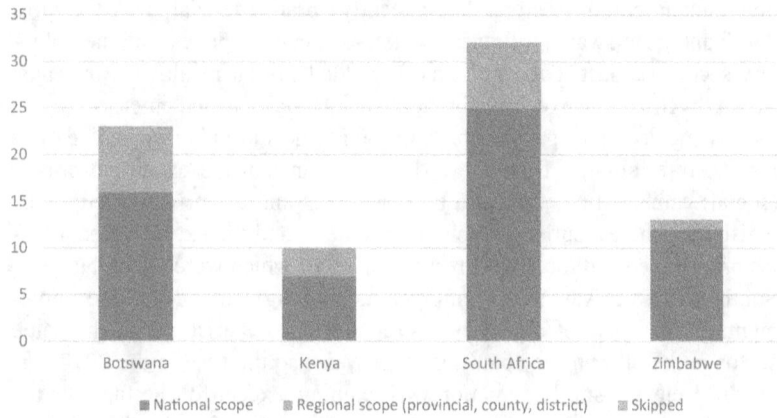

Figure 2.2 Scope of ERP and ECM deployment

Long description: Figure 2.2 Reveals that Botswana, Kenya, South Africa and Zimbabwe deployment of ERP and ECM systems in organisations that operated at two levels, namely those that operated on a national scale and those that operated on a regional scale.

on a regional scale. The majority of the infrastructure was deployed to organizations that operated on a national scale in all four cases. An identical survey administered in 2017 yielded similar results. This demonstrates that EPR and ECM systems can be implemented in organizations of any size and type. For example, Rajnoha et al. (2014) investigated implementation process improvements in medium to large companies in Slovakia, whereas Johansson (2004) focused on small- to medium-sized organizations, in a study titled *Exploring Application Service Provision: Adoption of the ASP concept for provision of ICTs in SMEs*. As a result, as organizations differ in size, so do their capabilities and resources, as well as their concerns about ERP (Uri Sørhellera, 2018).

Profession

This question sought to identify the general categories of study participants based on their broad job descriptions. The fact that the questionnaire was administered to the public sector in general made it necessary to appreciate the profiles of the respondents, given that the survey was anonymously distributed.

As indicated in Figure 2.3, the study participants belonged to only ten of the 20 professions listed in the survey questionnaire as technical services,

Digital records infrastructure 59

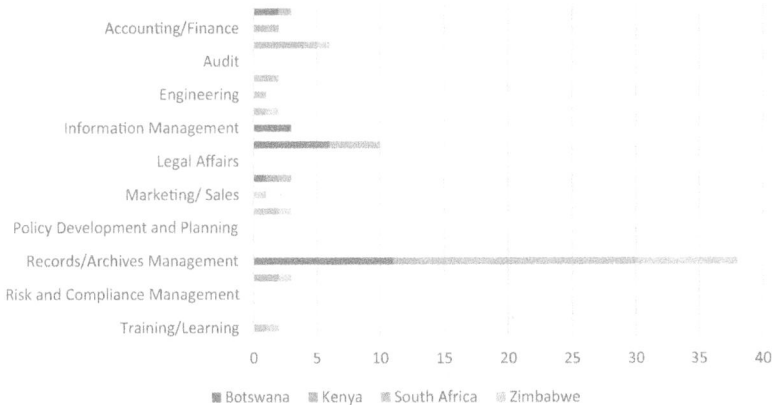

Figure 2.3 Participants by category

Long description: The Figure identifies the general categories of study participants based on their broad job descriptions. the study participants belonged to only ten of the twenty professions listed in the survey questionnaire as technical services, risk and compliance management, research, records/archives professionals, policy development and planning, operations, marketing/sales, legal affairs, information technology, human resources, communication/publications, audit, administration, accounting/finance, executive/senior management.

risk and compliance management, research, records/archives professionals, policy development and planning, operations, marketing/sales, legal affairs, information technology, human resources, communication/publications, auditing, administration, accounting/finance, and executive/senior management. Except for Kenya, the records/archives management profession dominated in Botswana, South Africa, and Zimbabwe.

Cloud computing use

Cloud computing services can be used for a variety of activities in organizations, including but not limited to those shown in Figure 2.4. Respondents were asked to select cloud computing applications that were relevant to their respective organizations. Among the options were driving business processing, security improvement, increasing collaboration, increasing organizational performance, increasing storage, keeping in pace with the industry, and cost reduction.

According to the data presented in Figure 2.4 from Botswana, South Africa, and Zimbabwe, a significant number of organizations to which the

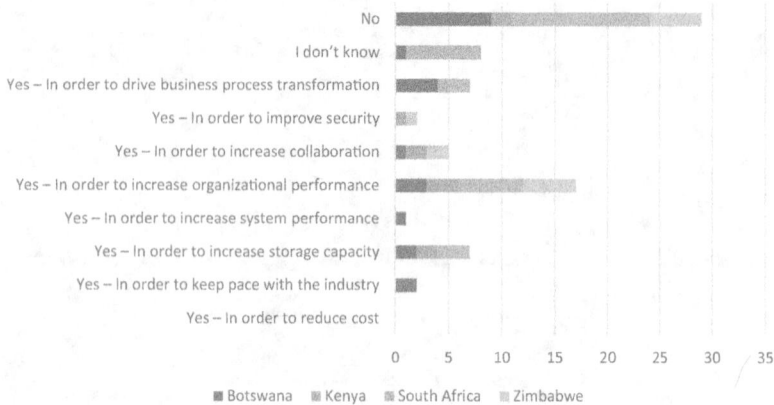

Figure 2.4 Cloud computing uses

Long description: Figure 2.4 shows that a significant number of organisations to which the respondents belonged did not use cloud computing in the management of their information assets.

respondents belonged did not use cloud computing in the management of their information assets. The 2017 survey yielded comparable results. Kenya received the highest number of responses in terms of using cloud computing services to improve organizational performance. Kenya's top responses in 2017 were to increase organizational performance and reduce costs. Although respondents in the current study were unable to identify the reasons for not adopting cloud computing in their respective organizations, Johansson et al. (2015) identified fear of losing control over data as the most important determinant of organizations' failure to adopt cloud computing services. This is because "in cloud-based ERPs, all organizational information, such as financial data and customer details, need to be stored with a third-party supplier" (Uri Sørhellera et al., 2018, p. 475). On the other hand, control regarding decreasing costs, as well as the inability of the organization to provide its own cloud computing service were some of the key determinants towards the adoption of cloud computing. Botswana emerged as the country in which cloud computing was used the most (with six uses recorded), followed by Kenya, which recorded four uses, while South Africa and Zimbabwe were trailing behind with only three uses recorded per country. However, the results were different from those of the 2017 survey, as both countries registered all six uses, albeit at varying levels. Contrary to the 2017 results, all four of the countries that were studied did not register using cloud computing for reducing costs associated with information management. On a good note, the deployment of cloud computing services to boost organizational performance emerged as ubiquitous use in the four countries. The same findings were obtained in 2017. This finding corroborates a previous study by Rajnoha et al. (2014), which was conducted in Slovakia, and which indicated that ERP systems did improve the competitiveness of organizations and supported the company's dynamics of development. Additionally, such systems were found to boost the return on investment in ERP systems, particularly for corporate executives and employees (Rajnoha et al., 2014).

Cloud computing service models

According to Johansson et al. (2015, p. 136), "the innovative part of cloud computing revolution is the consumerization of IT as a service which includes significant changes for consumers as well as for sellers." Given the availability of a variety of cloud service models on the market, respondents were asked to describe the types of service models used in their organizations.

Surprisingly, as reflected in Figure 2.5, the majority of respondents in Botswana, South Africa, and Zimbabwe were unaware of the service models in use in their organizations (similar results were obtained in 2017), while Kenya identified community cloud and hybrid models as its most commonly used models. This differs slightly from the 2017 results, in which Kenya recorded the private cloud as the model in use in their organizations, followed by the community cloud. On the one hand, hybrid cloud, private cloud, public cloud, and a combination of any two cloud computing service models were the models with the most widespread presence in all four countries, implying their popularity. Only South Africa, on the other hand, reported using a combination of all four service models. South Africa and Botswana emerged as the two countries with the most different models in use, with seven and six, respectively, with Kenya coming in third with four and Zimbabwe coming in last with only three. The results from the 2017 survey were slightly different. Then, the leading countries were Kenya and Botswana who recorded four service models, followed by Zimbabwe and South Africa, recording three and two service models, respectively.

Cloud computing deployment model

Users have a number of options or models to choose from when it comes to the deployment of cloud computing services. Question 6 of the survey instrument sought to understand the cloud deployment models used

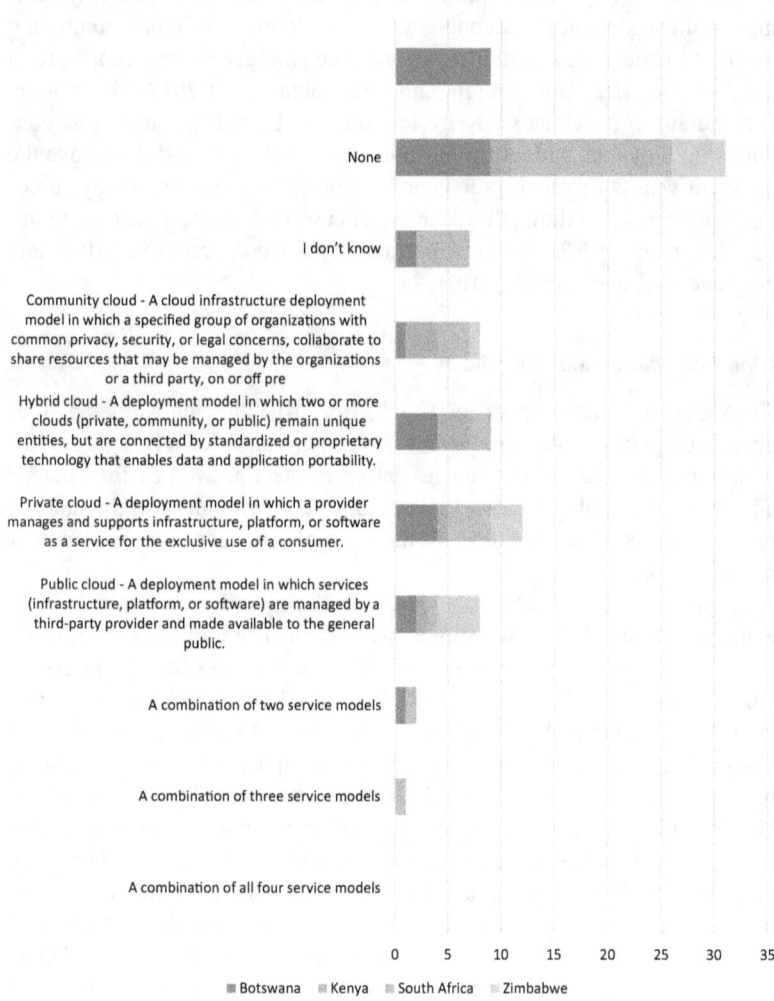

Figure 2.5 Cloud computing service models used

Long description: This Figure shows that the majority of respondents in Botswana, South Africa, and Zimbabwe were unaware of the service models in use in their organisations, while Kenya identified community cloud and hybrid models as its most commonly used models.

in various organizations across all four countries studied. According to Johansson et al. (2015), various cloud computing services have emerged over the years, with software as a service (SaaS) generating significant hype beginning in 2013. All of these technologies, however, were an extension of

Digital records infrastructure 63

the application services provisions (APS), which peaked in 2003, and they are fundamentally the same.

As was the case in 2017, a sizable proportion (28) of respondents from Botswana, South Africa, and Zimbabwe stated that none of the cloud computing services models listed in Question 6 of the survey instrument were in use at their institutions, while a sizable proportion (16) of participants from all four countries expressed ignorance about the model in use in their organizations (see Figure 2.6). However, all five models listed in the instrument were in use in some organizations in various countries that served as the study's research sites. Similar to the 2017 results, the platform as a service (PaaS) and SaaS models were the only ones that were present in

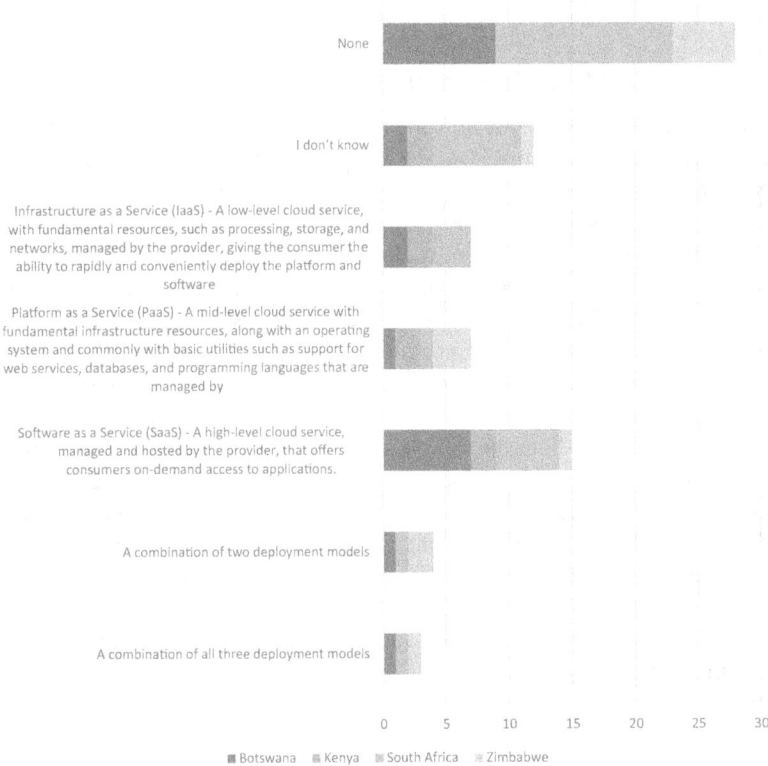

Figure 2.6 Cloud computing deployment model

Long description: Figure 2.6 shows that a sizable proportion (28) of respondents from Botswana, South Africa, and Zimbabwe stated that none of the cloud computing services models listed in question 6 of the survey instrument were in use at their institutions, while a sizable proportion (16) of participants from all four countries expressed ignorance about the model in use in their organisations

all four countries, with the other deployment models only being present in three. Botswana and South Africa had the most and the same number of deployment models, five, respectively, followed by Zimbabwe with four models and Kenya with three. In 2017, Kenya and Zimbabwe had the most models, with four, followed by Botswana and South Africa, each with three. In terms of prominence per deployment model in a country, SaaS led in Botswana and South Africa, while PaaS and infrastructure as a service (IaaS) had nearly equal shares in Kenya, with PaaS leading in Zimbabwe. The 2017 survey yielded similar results for Botswana and Zimbabwe, but different results for Kenya, where SaaS took the lead while IaaS was the highest in South Africa. Overall, the findings revealed that it was extremely uncommon for organizations to combine all three deployment models listed in the survey questionnaire.

Enterprise resource planning modules

Many organizations have implemented ERP packages dedicated to the management of their core business activities. ERP systems, according to Rajnoha et al. (2014), appear to be a pipe dream come true. "Each ERP module is designed for specific business functions, providing the data and supporting the processes that will help those employees do their jobs," notes McCue (2020). Each module in an ERP system plugs into the ERP system in such a way that the systems, including new modules, act as a single source of accurate information (McCue, 2020). This question sought to ascertain which ERP models had been implemented in the study's research sites.

As reflected in Figure 2.7, the accounting module was the most frequently reported module in both the 2017 and 2021 surveys. Manufacturing, marketing, and sales modules were reported to be the least used in 2017 and 2021, respectively. Botswana had the most modules (12), followed by South Africa with 11, and Zimbabwe and Kenya came in last with 10 and eight modules, respectively. In the 2017 survey, Botswana and Kenya produced similar results, while South Africa and Zimbabwe recorded 12 modules. The study's findings revealed that the four countries studied were making significant progress towards the realization of a total package of ERP modules, albeit at a slower pace.

Service providers

The common service providers in each country are reflected in Table 2.1.

The number of ERP and ECM system providers will always increase in lockstep with the level of information technology (IT) development around the world. South Africa and Botswana had the most ERP and ECM

Digital records infrastructure 65

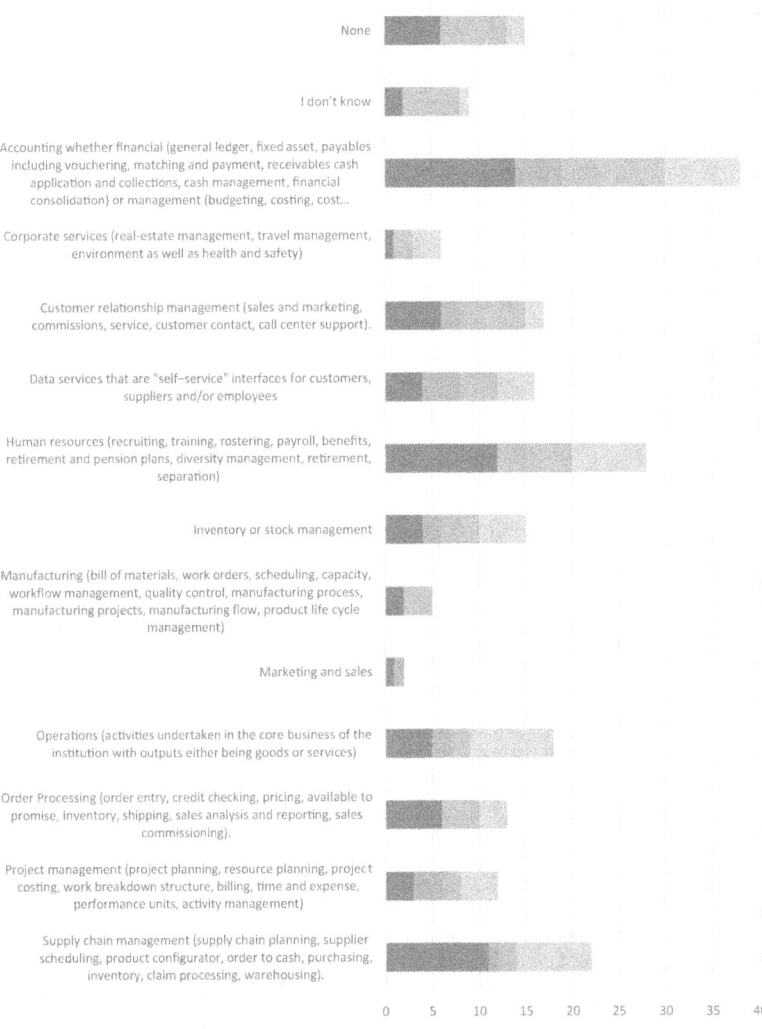

Figure 2.7 ERP modules deployed

Long description: Figure 2.7 shows that the accounting module was the most frequently reported module in both the 2017 and 2021 surveys.

Table 2.1 Service providers per country

COUNTRY	COMMON ERP SERVICE PROVIDERS	COMMON ECM SERVICE PROVIDERS
Botswana	1. SAP Success One 2. SAP Business One 3. Sage X3 4. Sage pastel 5. Sage ERP 300 6. Oracle People Soft 7. Oracle JD Edwards Enterprise One/World 8. Oracle E-Business Suite 9. Microsoft Dynamics 365 10. IFS Applications 11. IBM-Maximo 12. ITS	1. Alfresco 2. Hyland On-Base Suite 3. IBM (Content Foundation/ Manager aka Filnet) 4. M-Files 5. Microsoft SharePoint 2016 6. Microsoft SharePoint 2019 7. Microsoft SharePoint/Office 365 8. Open Text Livelink/Content Server/Suite 16
Kenya	1. IBM-Maximo 2. IFS Applications 3. IQMS 4. Microsoft Dynamics 365 5. Oracle E-Business	1. IBM (Content Foundation/ Manager aka Filnet) 2. Microsoft OneDrive 3. Microsoft SharePoint 2010 4. Microsoft SharePoint 2013 5. Microsoft SharePoint/Office 365
South Africa	1. IBM-Maximo 2. Microsoft Dynamics 365 3. Oracle E-Business 4. Oracle Fusion 5. Oracle Hyperiod 6. Oracle NetSuite 7. Sage Enterprise Management 8. Sage ERP 100 9. Sage ERP 300 10. Sage X3 11. SAP Business One 12. SAP Concur technologies 13. SAP Success Factors 14. SAP/4 HANA 15. Syspro	1. Afresco 2. Micro Focus Content Manager (Formerly HP Content Manager/ HP TRIM) 3. Microsoft OneDrive 4. Microsoft SharePoint 2010 5. Microsoft SharePoint 2013 6. Microsoft SharePoint 2016 7. Microsoft SharePoint 2019 8. Microsoft SharePoint/Office 365
Zimbabwe	1. IBM-Maximo 2. IFS Applications 3. IQMS 4. Microsoft Dynamics 365 5. Sage Intacct 6. Sage Enterprise Management 7. SAP Business One 8. SAP S/4 HANA 9. Ultimate Software	1. Micro Focus Content Manager (Formerly HP Content Manager/ HP TRIM) 2. Microsoft OneDrive 3. Microsoft SharePoint 2013 4. Microsoft SharePoint 2016 5. Microsoft SharePoint/Office 365 6. Open Text Documentum 7. Open Text Livelink/Content Server/Suite 8. Oracle Stellent/WebCentre

Long description: Table 2.1 reveals that South Africa and Botswana had the most ERP and ECM suppliers, with 15 and 12, respectively, while Zimbabwe trailed with nine. Kenya only registered five supplies. In 2017, Botswana registered 12 suppliers, Kenya registered eight suppliers, and South Africa and Zimbabwe registered six and three, respectively.

suppliers, with 15 and 12, respectively, while Zimbabwe trailed with nine. Kenya only registered five supplies. In 2017, Botswana registered 12 suppliers, Kenya registered eight suppliers, and South Africa and Zimbabwe registered six and three, respectively. The same pattern emerged in the 2021 survey results for ECM service providers, with South Africa leading the way, followed by Botswana, Zimbabwe, and, finally, Kenya. In 2017, South Africa led the way with eight ECM service providers, followed by Botswana, which reported five, and Kenya and Zimbabwe, which reported four and three, respectively. It is worth noting that some service providers, such as Microsoft, were present in all four countries. According to Tobie and Etoundi (2016), the most popular ERP suppliers in Africa are SAP, Oracle with PeopleSoft, and Infor with BaanMicrosoft. The number of service providers was generally satisfactory in all four countries, indicating healthy competition in the cloud computing industry. Many developing countries have turned into targets for ERP vendors, resulting in an increase in the number of ERP implementation projects.

Conclusion and recommendations

According to the findings of the study, ERP, ECM, and cloud computing technologies were gradually being rolled out in the four countries that comprised the study's population, albeit at a slightly slower pace. The study findings indicated that such technology deployment was in its early stages, with the potential for such technologies to become commonplace in the medium to long run, as supported by various ICT policies and legal frameworks that the four countries were implementing. The presence of seasoned service providers in all four countries was also a good indicator of a bright future, as such providers enable organizations to roll out ERP and ECM platforms. Overall, the digital records infrastructure in the four countries was in its infancy, and this differed from country to country, as evidenced by the study findings. Despite the slow pace of implementing or adopting the aforementioned technologies, the four countries appeared to be on a positive trajectory that should see most organizations roll out more of such systems in the future.

The study makes the following recommendations based on its findings:

1   There should be acceleration of ERP, ECM, and other cloud-based technologies that improve organizational performance.
2   Proactive electronic records management systems should be implemented prior to the implementation of such systems to ensure that commensurately sound electronic records management strategies are implemented to handle the resulting volumes of electronic content emanating from each system.

3 There should be promulgation of sound digital records management laws and policies that empower records and information practitioners to carry out sound records management practices, as such technologies present a new set of challenges to the records and information management fraternity.
4 Prior to their implementation, organizations should pay close attention to the selection and appraisal of ERP, ECM, and cloud computing services, ensuring that they retain complete control over the contents of such systems.
5 The long-term viability and stability of the various ERP, ECM, and cloud computing services that are being deployed should be ensured.
6 Interoperability standards should be leveraged for various ERP and ECM systems that are being rolled out to support and promote content sharing in increasingly networked environments.

References

Department of Communications and Digital Technologies. (2021). *Invitations to submit written submissions on the proposed national data and cloud computing*. Available at: https://www.gov.za/sites/default/files/gcis_document/202104/44389gon206.pdf

Fernandez, D., Zainol, Z. and Ahmad, H. (2017). 'The impacts of ERP systems on public sector Organizations,' *Procedia Computer Science*, 111, pp. 31–36.

Holland, C. P., Ben, L. and Nicola, G. (1999). 'A critical success factors model for enterprise resource planning implementation,' in *ECIS 1999: 7th European conference on information systems*, 23–25 June 1999. Available at: https://eprints.qut.edu.au/75692/1/ERP_CSF_-_ECIS99.pdf (Accessed 17 December 2017).

Johansson, B. (2004). 'Exploring application service provision: Adoption of the ASP concept for provision of ICTs in SMEs,' in J. Damasgaard and H. Z. Henriksen, *IFP TC88/WG8.6 Working conference on the diffusion and adoption of networked information technologies*, October 6–8, 2003, Copenhagen, Denmark, pp. 153–166. Available at: https://link.springer.com/content/pdf/10.1007%2F1-4020-7862-5_9.pdf (Accessed 2 August 2021).

Johansson, B., Ruivo, P. and Rodrigues, J. (2015). 'Adoption reasons for enterprise systems as service – a recap of provider perspectives,' *Procedia Computer Science*, 64, pp. 132–139.

Katuu, S. (2012). 'Enterprise Content Management (ECM) implementation in South Africa,' *Records Management Journal*, 22 (1), pp. 37–56.

Katuu, S. (2020). 'Enterprise resource planning: Past, present, and future,' *New Review of Information Networking*, 25, pp. 1, 37–46. https://doi.org/10.1080/13614576.2020

Khanda, M. and Doss, S. (2018). 'SME cloud adoption in Botswana: Its challenges and successes,' *International Journal of Advanced Computer Science and Applications*, 9 (1), pp. 468–478

Maseh, E. (2015). *Records management readiness for open government in the Kenyan Judiciary*. University of KwaZulu-Natal, Pietermaritzburg. PhD thesis.
McCue, I. (2020). *ERP modules: Types, features & functions*. Available at: www.netsuite.com/portal/resource/articles/erp/erp-modules.shtml (Accessed 2 August 2021).
Moatlhodi, T. M. (2015). *An assessment of e-records readiness at the Ministry of Labor and Home Affairs Headquarters in Botswana*. University of Botswana, Botswana. Master's thesis.
Mosweu, O. (2018). *A framework to authenticate records in a government accounting system in Botswana to support the auditing process*. University of South Africa, Pretoria. PhD thesis.
Mosweu, T., Luthuli, L. and Mosweu, O. (2019). 'Implications of cloud-computing services in records management in Africa: Achilles heels of the digital era?' *South African Journal of Information Management*, 21 (1), pp. 10–69.
Mosweu, O. and Ngoepe, M. (2021). 'Trustworthiness of digital records in government accounting system to support the audit process in Botswana,' *Records Management Journal*, 31 (1), pp. 89–108.
Nengomasha, C. T. and Chikomba, A. (2018). 'Status of EDRMS implementation in the public sector in Namibia and Zimbabwe,' *Records Management Journal*, 28 (3), pp. 252–264.
Ngoepe, M. (2015). 'Deployment of open source electronic content management software in national government departments in South Africa,' *Journal of Science & Technology Policy Management*, 6 (3), pp. 190–205. http://dx.doi.org/10.1108/JSTPM-05-2014-0021
Ngoepe, M. (2017). 'Archival orthodoxy of post-custodial realities for digital records in South Africa,' *Archives and Manuscripts*, 45 (1), pp. 31–44.
Rajnoha, R., Kádárová, J., Sujová, A. and Kádár, G. (2014). 'Business information systems: Research study and methodological proposals for ERP implementation process improvement,' *Procedia – Social and Behavioral Sciences*, 109, pp. 165–170.
Republic of Kenya. (2019). *Digital economy blueprint: Powering Kenya's transformation*. Available at: www.ict.go.ke/wp-content/uploads/2019/05/Kenya-Digital-Economy-2019.pdf (Accessed 17 December 2021).
ResearchICTafrica.net. (2017). *Drivers and barriers for cloud computing adoption in the public sector in Kenya*. Available at: https://researchictafrica.net/ria_rap/2017/11/22/drivers-and-barriers-for-cloud-computing-adoption-in-the-public-sector-in-kenya/
Shibambu, A. and Marutha, N. S. (2021). 'A framework for management of digital records on the cloud in the public sector of South Africa,' *Information Discovery and Delivery*, Vol. ahead-of-print No. ahead-of-print. https://doi.org/10.1108/IDD-10-2020-0128
Shibambu, A. and Ngoepe, M. (2020). 'When rain clouds gather: Digital curation of South African public records in the cloud,' *South African Journal of Information Management*, 22 (1). https://doi.org/10.4102/sajim.v22i1.1205
Sigauke, D. T. and Nengomasha, C. T. (2012). 'Challenges and prospects facing the digitization of historical records for their preservation within the National

Archives of Zimbabwe,' *Paper Presented at the ICADLA 2: International Conference on African Digital Libraries and Archives*, University of Witwatersrand, Johannesburg, South Africa.

Tobie, A. M. and Etoundi, R. S. (2016). 'A literature review of ERP implementation in African countries,' *Electronic Journal of Information Systems in Developing Countries*, 76 (4), pp. 1–20. Available at: https://onlinelibrary.wiley.com/doi/pdf/10.1002/j.1681-4835.2016.tb00555.x (Accessed 2 August 2021).

Tsai, W., Lee, P., Shen, Y. and Lin, H. (2012). 'A comprehensive study of the relationship between enterprise resource planning selection criteria and enterprise resource planning system success,' *Information & Management*, 49, pp. 36–46. https://doi.org/10.1016/j.im.2011.09.007

Uri Sørhellera, V., Høvika, E. J., Hustada, E. and Vassilakopouloua, P. (2018). 'Implementing cloud ERP solutions: A review of sociotechnical concerns,' *Procedia Computer Science*, 138, pp. 470–477.

Walwyn, D. R. and Cloete, L. (2020). 'South Africa has failed to harness the digital revolution: How it can fix the problem,' *The Conversation*. Available at: https://theconversation.com/south-africa-has-failed-to-harness-the-digital-revolution-how-it-can-fix-the-problem-147799 (Accessed 18 December 2021).

3 Authentication of records for auditing processes

Mpho Ngoepe, Jonathan Mukwevho, and Olefhile Mosweu

Introduction

Proper records management enables accounting officers to furnish the public audit oversight system, such as the Auditor General of South Africa (AGSA) with accurate, reliable, and authentic records of financial statements for auditing (Mosweu, 2018). The AGSA's preventative control guides were developed to enable accounting officers or authorities to effectively address the assurance needs of oversight structures on preventive controls. They give special importance to proper record-keeping in ensuring that transactions are processed in a complete, accurate, and timely manner and that authentic and accurate records are available to support financial reporting (AGSA, 2020a). The AGSA's preventative control guides further stipulate that records used for processing transactions should be kept in an orderly filing or records management system to allow for easy retrieval during the performance of checks and reviews by those assigned the responsibility of monitoring accounting and reporting activities (AGSA, 2020b). However, when releasing the 2019–20 general report for national and provincial governments, the AGSA (2021) cited widespread weaknesses in basic internal controls. Such weaknesses included proper record-keeping, with only 61 out of 146 (42%) auditees providing evidence of good controls. Examples of control include protective mechanisms in place to prevent the alteration, loss, corruption, or destruction of records; controlled access to records; documented authentication; and approval mechanisms for records, among others (Ngoepe and Mukwevho, 2018). Due to poor records management practices, most auditees appeared to be making untrustworthy and unreliable information available to external public auditors, who are independent of the public institution being audited, during the audit process (AGSA, 2021).

Increased digital transformation further presents distinctive challenges for the government to retain the authenticity of digital records because, unlike physical records, they can easily be corrupted, resulting in digital records

DOI: 10.4324/9781003203155-4

losing their trustworthiness. There are no guidelines with clear-cut criteria that auditors can use to judge whether digital records are authentic and reliable to support the audit process (Ngoepe and Ngulube, 2014). As a result, auditors often do not accept digital records as evidence due to a lack of measurement of trustworthiness (Mosweu and Ngoepe, 2021). This chapter discusses authentication of records in the digital environment to support the audit process, with the view of exploring the development of guidelines that auditors may use to determine the authenticity of digital records tendered as evidence in the audit process. In this regard, risks related to digital records and the management of these records are presented. Furthermore, the trustworthiness of digital records as audit evidence is discussed. Despite the fact that the AGSA is the case study for digital records authentication to support the audit process, the recommendations in this chapter can be applied broadly to other organizations to ensure accurate and authentic digital records.

Trustworthiness of digital records

Authentication in archival terms means that the record can be proven to be what it purports to be when created or sent by the person who created or sent it, and to have been created or sent at the time it is purported to have been created or sent (Duranti, 2010). It is an authentication certification or verification based on material proof, inferences, or deductions. A record can be wittingly or unwittingly altered, affecting its authenticity. Alterations in the digital environment are preventable through permission, access control, and verifiable methods like checksum, a unique fingerprint of a file that can be used to verify whether two files are identical, and blockchain technology designed to confirm records' integrity, existence at a certain point in time, and sequence to support their non-repudiation (Stancic et al., 2020). In the manual environment, Ngoepe (2012) reports of situations where auditees have created records to satisfy an audit query. In this regard, when auditors require supporting documentation, the auditees would call the service provider to supply an invoice created at the time the audit query was made and not at the time the transaction took place. In this instance, while the archival bond of this invoice and related documents is questionable, the authenticity of the invoice was never verified but only accepted by auditors based on its correctness. Similarly, with logs in the digital environment, such a record can be declared untrustworthy. Therefore, it becomes important for auditors to understand that the archival bond is fundamental to the record, and without it, records would not exist. An archival bond exists when there is an interrelationship between a record and others, resulting from the same activity (Pearce-Moses, 2005). To support trustworthiness, the chain of legitimate custody, that is, a ground for inferring reliability and trustworthiness of the document trail, is essential. Similarly, the digital chain of custody (the information preserved about the document and its changes that shows that specific data was in a specific state at a given date and time) must be maintained. One method is to have an expert issue a declaration that bases the trustworthiness of digital documents on the effective management of an electronic records management system where records are hosted, as well as institutional procedures and processes in place to control the preservation and use of digital records (Duranti, 2010; Duranti and Jansen, 2011).

The records on which the creator relies in the normal and ordinary course of business are presumed authentic in both archival theory and jurisprudence (Duranti and Blanchette, 2004). As a result, when it comes to keeping records in digital systems, the presumption of authenticity must be supported by evidence that a record is what it claims to be and has not been altered by unauthorized parties. In order to assess the authenticity of a digital record, the preserver must be able to establish its identity and demonstrate its identity and integrity. A record's identity refers to distinguishing characteristics that are unique to a record; that is, the attributes of a record that uniquely characterize it and distinguish it from other records (InterPARES, 2002). From an archival diplomatic perspective, such attributes include names, dates, actions/matters, archival bonds, and attachments, if any. The identity of a record is constituted by all of these characteristics, which distinguish it from any other record, and it is judged based on the formal elements embedded in the record, and/ or its attributes, as expressed, through, for example, metadata (Pearce-Moses, 2019, p. 275; Duranti, 2010, p. 15). A record has integrity if the message it is meant to communicate to achieve its purpose is complete and uncorrupted in all its essential respects for the duration of its existence (Duranti, 2010, p. 16; InterPARES, 2002, p. 2). In addition, an unbroken chain of responsible and legitimate custody of records is considered insurance of integrity until proof is given to the contrary. Integrity metadata is required to attest to that. Alternatively, a record can be declared authentic if the integrity of the records and information management system in which it is created, received, or stored can be proven, including the reliability of its recordkeeping process (National Standard of Canada, 2017). Hence, the quality of the reliability of the system operated properly to produce a record is a measure of the quality of the record's evidential value, which, in turn, is a measure of the record's integrity (Ma et al., 2009). The legislative framework also plays an important role in authenticating records. The following subsection presents the legislative framework and standards for authentic records.

Legislative framework and standards for authentic records

As records management systems transact organizational business, a strong legislative framework is required for the management and maintenance of authentic and reliable digital records produced by records management systems (Mosweu, 2018, p. 175). As discussed in Chapter 1, the Electronic Communication and Transaction Act (ECTA) (No. 25 of 2002) in South Africa establishes legislative requirements to ensure that the reliability and authenticity of digital records are given due evidential weight. According to the ECTA, the evidential weight of digital records is comparable to that of paper-based records as long as certain requirements are met. In accordance with Section 15(3) of the ECTA, the following factors must be considered when determining the evidential weight of a data message (digital records):

- the reliability of the manner in which the data message was generated, stored, or communicated;
- the reliability of the manner in which the integrity of the data message was maintained;
- the manner in which its originator was identified; and
- any other relevant factor.

Furthermore, the ECTA does not prohibit a person or organization from establishing requirements for the way that an organization, in this case the AGSA, will accept digital records. For example, Section 27 of ECTA stipulates that:

> Any public body, in pursuant of any law accepts the filing of documents, or requires that documents be created or retained ... may notwithstanding anything to the contrary in such law accept the filing of such documents or the creation or retention of such documents in the form of data messages (digital records).

Section 28 (1) further states,

> such body may specify by notice in the Gazette –
>
> (a) the manner and format in which the data messages must be filed, created, retained or issued;
> (b) in cases where the data message has to be signed, the type of electronic signature required;
> (c) the manner and format in which such electronic signature must be attached to, incorporated in or otherwise associated with the data message;
> (d) the identity of or criteria that must be met by any authentication service provider used by the person filing the data message or that such authentication service provider must be a preferred authentication service provider;

(e) the appropriate control process and procedures to ensure adequate integrity, security and confidentiality of data messages ... and
(f) any other requirements for data messages.

The requirements specified previously are applicable to this chapter, and the key principles required to determine the trustworthiness of digital records are as follows:

1. It should have been generated during the regular course of business activities.
2. Standard processes and procedures are adhered to when capturing, transmitting, and storing electronic information.
3. Integrity of the system capturing, transmitting, and storing digital information is maintained at all times.

More importantly, the National Archives and Records Service of South Africa Act (No. 43 of 1996 as amended) empowers the National Archivist to decide how digital records systems should be controlled and administered. The National Archives and Records Service of South Africa (NARSSA) assisted the South African Bureau of Standards in the adoption of SANS 15801 as a national standard: Electronic Imaging – Information stored electronically – Recommendations for trustworthiness and reliability as a South African national standard because the ECTA does not stipulate the specific requirements that would allow one to prove the integrity and reliability of records (National Archives and Records Services of South Africa, 2006, p. 26). South African National Standard 15801 (2013) specifies the methods for storing all types of digital information in an authentic and dependable manner. However, this does not imply that authenticating digital records is automatic and can be satisfied solely by adhering to this standard. Capra (2017, p. 3) states that in the legal context, digital records can present the challenge of convincing court officials that they have not been altered or hacked, and that they came from specified sources. As a result of this challenge, the South African Law Reform Commission advocates for a clearer articulation of both statutory and non-statutory (handbook/manual) guidelines for the authentication (and weight) of documentary evidence, particularly electronic evidence (South African Law Reform Commission, 2019, p. 62). From an audit perspective, the guidelines are necessary to set forth factors that auditors may consider when authenticating digital records presented by government records and information management systems during the audit process. When checking and reviewing the financial management and financial statements of public institutions, audit firms, particularly the AGSA, use a risk-based approach to ensure that they audit what matters. The section that follows describes a risk-based approach to records management that ensures authentic digital records are generated and retained in government records and information management systems.

Risks affecting the authenticity of records

From a records management perspective, risk relates to challenges to the trustworthiness of the records, including litigation risk, which can be expected over the life of the record, and unauthorized loss or destruction of records (National Archives and Records Administration, 2005, p. 1). The authenticity of technology-generated digital records, including email messages, is at great risk whenever they are transmitted between systems or when the hardware or software used to store, process, and communicate them is updated or replaced (Stancic et al. 2019, p. 139; Mosweu, 2018, p. 75). In addition, the government's inability to reconstruct views of web content that was created dynamically could create a challenge for citizens when the trustworthiness of the website-related records could not be verified or if there was unauthorized loss or destruction (National Archives and Records Administration, 2005, p. 1).

A risk-based approach to records management identifies, prevents, mitigates, and effectively constrains threats to an acceptable level, thereby minimizing potential losses of authenticity (Erima and Wamukoya, 2012, p. 27). There is no denying that digital information technology creates significant risks, including risks related to the management of email messages, websites records, and social media records and the risk that digital records may be altered, either accidentally or maliciously, as a result, reducing the quality and integrity of those records (InterPARES, 2002, p. 1; Mosweu, 2018, p. 75). For instance, in the media statement on the Experian security breach in August 2020, the Information Regulator for South Africa expressed her concern about the alleged security breach experienced by Experian South Africa, which compromised the personal information of reportedly 24 million South Africans due to a fraudulent misrepresentation that occurred in May 2020 (Information Regulator South Africa, 2020, p. 1). This poses the challenge of convincing someone that such digital records have not been altered. In addition, media reports indicate that the government struggled to authenticate the Guptas' (an Indian-born South African business family whose most notable members are the brothers Ajay, Atul, and Rajesh) leaked emails. A series of explosive emails showed the extent of the Gupta family's control over cabinet ministers and state-owned companies, and their CEOs and boards. The authenticity of the emails has been questioned by some people as they argue that former President Jacob Zuma's faction and the Gupta family were buying time hoping the government could set up a judicial commission of inquiry. The National Prosecuting Authority further sought to independently authenticate evidence contained in the leaked Gupta emails to account for how they obtained the emails, where they received the emails from, and what the chain of custody was. Another situation where the authenticity of cellphone records was questioned was in the case of *Oscar Pistorius* (a South African sprinter who made history in 2012 as the first amputee to compete in track events at the Olympics and was found guilty of murdering his girlfriend on Valentine's Day 2013) *versus the State of South Africa* (Ngoepe and Mukwevho, 2018, p. 7). All of the previous examples provide a glimpse into how the authenticity of digital records could be compromised.

Risks pertaining to malicious alteration can be mitigated through permission and access controls (i.e., details of all levels of access available in the system and procedures for their use). Additional hardware and/or software is required to be more effective. For instance, fog and edge computing seeks to provide minimum computing, storage, and networking resources at the edge of the network for quick processing of digital information. Proper authentication of fog and edge nodes and secure communication protocols could help provide a minimum level of security to ensure integrity and authenticity at the fog and edge layers (Hurbungs et al., 2021, p. 9). In addition, one cannot rely on file size, dates, or other file properties, but rather on audit logs and strong methods like checksums and blockchains (Duranti and Rogers, 2012, p. 526). Suffice to say, checksums and blockchains validate the integrity and identity of digital records and are used for a variety of applications, including digital signatures and user identification and authentication. Another form of authenticating digital records is through metadata. Ma et al. (2009, p. 3) argue that when a person needs to determine a record's trustworthiness, they need to first find metadata about the record. It is through the presence of metadata that particular resources can act as authoritative evidence of business actions. This involves records being sustainable over application system boundaries in ways that render them usable and interpretable for as long as they are required (Mosweu, 2018, p. 74). Therefore, it is the responsibility of all government institutions to ensure that proper metadata (a set of data that describes and gives information about other data) and audit trail data (a record of the changes that have been made to a database or file) are captured, and a digital signature, where necessary, is incorporated into a digital file to prove the authenticity and reliability of the digital records as evidence of transactions. This chapter considers metadata, audit trails, and a digital signature as the methods to ensure the authentication of records. If properly implemented and maintained, they can serve as a mitigation factor for risk associated with the creation, storage, and transmission of digital records by government records management systems.

Trustworthiness of digital records as audit evidence

This section first describes the audit process and then discusses the relationship between the audit process and authentic digital records, because authentic digital records are a critical means by which organizations preserve evidence to support the audit process, without which a disclaimer of opinion can be issued to the government institution due to insufficient evidence provided to auditors in the form of documentation. Finally, it provides an overview of guidelines for assessing authentic digital records during the audit process.

Audit process

The AGSA was established as the supreme audit institution in terms of the Republic of South Africa's Constitution of 1996. Its purpose is to promote accountability and improve the reliability and authenticity of financial reports by auditing and reporting on the accounts, financial statements, and financial management of the public sector. Financial laws in South Africa, such as the Public Financial Management Act (No. 1 of 1999), generally require government departments to ensure that financial and accounting records are kept and managed adequately. According to South African audit legislation such as the Public Audit Act (No. 25 of 2004), authorized public auditors have full access to digital records as audit evidence when conducting an audit. Section 52 of the AGSA directive – No. 41321 gazetted on 17 December 2017 – issued in terms of the Public Audit Act, 2004, describes all documentation and information the public entities must make available for audit purposes. These include, for instance, asset documentation such as asset registers, predetermined information such as strategic plans, human resource records such as leave files, minutes of meetings of selection committees, supply chain records such as payment batches, as well as tender documents (Stancic et al., 2019, p. 141). Similarly, directives issued from time to time by the AGSA may include requirements for how it will accept digital records in accordance with the ECTA. In addition, an auditor must consider all available documentation and information as part of the assurance process leading to an audit opinion (Organisation for Economic Co-operation and Development, 2004, p. 8; ISA 500, 2009, p. 382). Simply stated, the auditor must be assured that the data, in this case, financial information, produced by the government records and information management systems is accurate, reliable, and complete (Cain and Brech, 1999, p. 90) to fulfil the requirements of the external public auditors.

In the South African context, the Cabinet's approved Integrated Financial Management System should be implemented by national and provincial departments, which replaced several transversal systems in the areas of supply chain management, human resource management, financial management, payroll, and business intelligence (National Treasury, 2021, p. 1). However, there is always a challenge when many countries' government entities have to implement electronic content management (ECM) systems, while others have enterprise resource planning (ERP) systems, and still others generate digital records without the benefit of any controlled system (Stancic et al., 2019, p. 137). Using uncontrolled records and information management systems to share and transmit financial records during the COVID-19 pandemic further created the risk that untrustworthy information could be accessed and used during the audit process. Moreover, the use of uncontrolled records and information management systems such as shared drives and Microsoft SharePoint (AGSA, 2020b) created a small step towards remote auditing, if not hybrid auditing. Shneyder (2020) refers to remote auditing where audits are performed virtually rather than on-site. Due to the COVID-19 pandemic, the need for virtual audits was accelerated (KPMG, 2020) because of health protocols such as social distancing.

Over time, auditors have used information and communication technologies (ICTs) to accrue benefits from their usage, enabling them to extend their scope, change the timing, and reduce the cost of the audit process (Teeter et al., 2010). For example, accounting systems such as ERP systems bring more efficiency into the audit process, although that also depends on the quality of the ERP systems (Caringe and Holm, 2017). Accounting information generated in an ERP system can be validated through an integrated ECM-ERP system with the accurate data archived in the ECM system (Nissen, 2018). Using computer assisted audit techniques (CAATs) has also led to improvements in the quality of audit reports (Omonuk, 2015). Therefore, technological advancements have made remote or virtual auditing much easier, and have improved audit procedures.

Audit process and authentic digital records

The widespread migration of financial information, accounting records, and audit evidence to digital media may be cause for concern, because many auditors do not exercise caution when evaluating digital audit evidence. This could be due to the fact that, to some extent, external public auditors are not effectively trained to collect and evaluate digital audit evidence, nor have they learnt how to do so in practice (Nearon, 2005, p. 34). As a result, according to the INTOSAI Capacity Building Committee's (2020, p. 16) paper on the future relevant and value-adding auditor, auditors must remain curious and willing to learn as new technologies and methods emerge. Auditors should also be prepared to build their own capacity regarding digital literacy. Finally, digital signatures present a challenge for auditors because no evidence exists to validate the purpose of the signer of a specific document (Caster and Verardo, 2007, p. 70).

Due to situations like the ones mentioned previously, external public auditors may not accept digital records as evidence during the audit cycle.

Consequently, many records management professionals lament that auditors, especially in the digital periphery, do not always accept digital records as evidence to support the audit queries due to a lack of guidelines for their authentication (Mosweu, 2011, p. 110; Ngoepe and Mukwevho, 2018, p. 8; Stancic et al., 2019, p. 139). Therefore, it is important to consider the ability for government organizations to do business completely electronically, in conjunction with new business methods and models (Organisation for Economic Co-operation and Development, 2004, p. 6). Section 27 of the ECTA provides a legislative framework for the government to conduct business (make or receive payment) in electronic form or by electronic means.

An advance electronic signatures forms an important part of the audit trail for e-government business transactions and will be of considerable value to both public and private auditors (Organisation for Economic Co-operation and Development, 2004, p. 11). Law Trust Party Services (Pty) Ltd (law trust) and the South African Post Office Ltd (SAPO trust centre) are the accredited authentication and certification products and services in support of an advance electronic signature by the South African Accreditation Authority in terms of Section 37 of the ECTA (South African Accreditation Authority, 2020, p. 1). Therefore, control documents generated in a purchase ordering process could be used to support the authenticity of the origin and integrity of the invoice, if government departments can demonstrate a high level of integrity in their electronic system in which techniques such as an advanced electronic signatures, metadata, and audit trails could authenticate the documents, as revealed earlier in this chapter. Using these types of techniques can enable both private and public auditors to obtain levels of assurance with respect to the reliability of invoices and financial statements available in digital format (Organisation for Economic Co-operation and Development, 2004, p. 12). Therefore, it becomes important that the envisaged guidelines should incorporate these techniques in one way or the other.

Guidelines to assess authentic digital records during the audit process

The AGSA conducts financial information audits in accordance with International Standards on Auditing (ISAs) (Auditor General of South Africa, 2017, p. 45). The ISAs provide some guidance to help the auditor decide whether the audit evidence required is sufficient and appropriate. The ISAs do not specify how much evidence must be gathered or the quality of that evidence. According to Mentz et al. (2018, p. 2), the basis for determining "sufficient appropriate evidence" is thus determined by the auditor's professional judgement, which may mean that there is little consistency regarding the quantity and quality of audit evidence obtained, particularly where auditors are inexperienced or lack the necessary skills to evaluate evidence provided during the audit process. The authors also stated that audit quality was not improving in areas where the auditor must exercise judgement (Mentz et al., 2018, vp. 2).

The question is, "How can audit quality be improved in areas where the auditor must exercise judgement?" According to Ma et al. (2009, p. 2) and Pearce-Moses (2005, p. 152), for a record to be accepted as credible evidence, metadata must be incorporated in a way that can be inspected, validated, and reasoned about by authorized users, allowing them to check and ensure that records have not been modified, abused, or tampered with. As part of their strategic records management policy, the NARSSA (2006, p. i) adopted the SANS 23081-part 1–2 standard to provide guidance to public institutions in designing a metadata capturing and management strategy. From an audit perspective, such metadata and audit logs can help external public auditors obtain trustworthy audit evidence to reduce audit risk to an acceptable level, allowing them to draw reasonable conclusions on which to base an audit opinion (Mentz et al., 2018, p. 2). Mentz et al. (2018, p. 2) added that there is a need to develop and communicate overarching principles to guide auditors in making these decisions. Furthermore, Stancic et al. (2019, p. 140) propose a framework that cannot be easily operationalized in the absence of appropriate guidelines for auditors to use in determining the authenticity of digital records made available during the audit process. Table 3.1 demonstrates that, despite the existence of legislation in the form of the ECTA, there are no guidelines that auditors can use to determine the authenticity of digital records presented during the audit process.

Table 3.1 demonstrates that both public institutions and external public auditors are aware of the impact of technological advancements on their business operations. Trust in the information and records presented by this technology appears to be a root cause of their inability to understand each other, which is exacerbated by a lack of trustworthiness measurements.

Therefore, it becomes imperative to develop the guidelines and checklists that public auditors can use to determine the trustworthiness of the audit evidence in any format, to conclude that the public can trust the evidence. The guidelines have been developed and attached as Annexure A, supported by the checklist available on InterPARES Website. Generally, the guidelines require the external public auditor to first ask the information systems auditor (combines the analytical skills of an auditor with the technology expertise of information technology) to assess the information systems environment in which the government records and information management systems operate to determine whether reliance can be placed on the general controls surrounding the system. The guidelines further indicate that after the general control environment of the government institution has been assessed and the

Table 3.1 Evidence of lack of guidelines for authenticating digital records for auditing

PARTICIPANTS	DATA COLLECTION METHODS/TOOLS	STATEMENTS
Government institutions/ auditees	AGSA's annual RM seminar	"The evolution of records and document management, digitisation and paperless, e-DRMS is now the future, will the AGSA accept e-DRMS?" "Auditors do not accept electronically scanned records."
An audit manager	Interview	"The auditor can accept digital information if certain criteria are met."
Auditor	Knowledge sharing session	"How do you know that the contract has been back dated?"
Senior auditor	Interview	"We need the records of the decision which was made prior to when the action took place?"

key internal controls found to be operating effectively, the digital records authentication checklist should be completed to assess the authenticity and reliability of the digital records that are stored or created on the government records and information systems. The guidelines have been reviewed and revised by the information systems auditor based on her working experience and knowledge in auditing in the South African public sector.

Finally, the authors gained insights from this study that can be summarized as follows:

- Trustworthy records are authentic and reliable. This can be accomplished through the use of techniques such as advanced electronic signatures, metadata, and audit trails.
- Authenticity refers to the identity and integrity of a record. This can be accomplished by utilizing technologies such as blockchain, checksum, and the hash algorithm.
- The ECTA provides a legislative framework for the originality, integrity, reliability, and admissibility of digital records, in this case, during the audit process, which can be supplemented by guidelines and checklists with specific requirements that allow one to prove the integrity and reliability of records.
- SANS 15801 specifies best practices for determining the trustworthiness of digital records. The guidelines include an assessment of the system's

general controls and the completion of an authentication checklist to determine the authenticity and reliability of the digital records.
- The degree of trustworthiness is determined by examining the completeness of the record's form as well as the amount of control exercised over the process of its creation.
- Metadata and audit trail data provide the historical information required to assess the trustworthiness of digital information, the specifics of which can be included in the guidelines.
- A digital signature that includes a checksum and hash value attached to a file allows the origin and integrity of the record to be verified. Digital signatures accomplish this verification by demonstrating that a digital message or document has not been altered, either intentionally or unintentionally, from the time it was signed.
- The ISA does not specify how much evidence must be obtained or its credibility, so guidelines for how much evidence must be captured become important.

Conclusion

The purpose of this chapter was to investigate the development of guidelines/ checklists for authenticating the integrity and reliability of digital records generated in government records and information management systems. For digital records, unlike paper records, it may be difficult or impossible to determine the authorship, provenance, or chain of custody because they can be easily transmitted, shared, and copied, especially on a less controlled or informal system such as shared drives. Authentication methods include relevant legislation, standards, metadata, audit trails, and a digital signature. Furthermore, the COVID-19 audit allowed auditors to remotely check and review documentation shared via uncontrolled records and information management systems like shared drives and Microsoft SharePoint. As a result of the lack of guidelines to supplement and operationalize the proposed framework, auditors find it difficult to mitigate the risks associated with the authenticity of digital records, as pointed out earlier in this chapter.

Therefore, it is suggested that the guidelines derived from the proposed framework (see Annexure A) be piloted with a few auditees for validation. The AGSA may issue a notice in the Government Gazette outlining how digital records will be accepted as evidence in the audit process. External public auditors should also be trained in records management processes and how to determine the authenticity of digital records. Alternatively, during the audit cycle, records management officials should be included on the audit team. Finally, it is recommended that the audit system of external public auditors be integrated with government records and information management systems, taking security and level of restrictions into account, so that authorized auditors can be granted access to and can review ERP or ECM documents and records online – a step towards the future, relevant, value-adding auditor facilitating remote auditing.

This study suggests future qualitative research on the practical implementation of the guidelines and checklist to assess the authenticity and reliability of digital records provided by government institutions during the audit process.

References

Auditor General of South Africa. (2017). 'Directive issued in terms of the Public audit Act, 2004,' *Government Gazette*, No. 41321.15 December 2017, pp. 43–79. Pretoria: Government Printers.

Auditor General of South Africa. (2020a) *Preventative control guides: Preparation of financial statements: Guide 5*. Available at: www.agsa.co.za/Portals/0/AuditInfo/Preventative%20guide/Preventative%20 control%20guide%205.pdf (Accessed 22 April 2021).

Auditor General of South Africa. (2020b). *First special report on the financial management of government's covid-19 initiatives*. Available at: www.agsa.co.za/Portals/0/Reports/Special%20Reports/Covid-19%20Special% 20report/Special%20 report%20interactive%20_final.pdf (Accessed 13 June 2021).

Auditor General of South Africa. (2021). *Media release: Auditor general calls on government leaders to ensure 'sustainable' audit outcomes*. Available at: www.agsa.co.za/Portals/0/Reports/PFMA/201920/2021%20PFMA%20Media%20 Release%20FINALISED%202.pdf (Accessed 22 April 2021).

Cain, P. and Brech, D. (1999). *Managing public sector records: Managing financial records*. Roper, M. and Laura Millar, L. (eds.). London: International Records Management Trust.

Capra, D. (2017). *Authenticating digital evidence*. Bronx: Fordham University.

Caringe, A. and Holm, E. (2017). *The auditor's role in a digital world – empirical evidence on auditors' perceived role and its implications on the principal-agent justification*. Available at: www.diva-portal.org/smash/get/diva2:1111236/FULLTEXT01. pdf (Accessed 12 January 2021).

Caster, P. and Verardo, D. (2007). 'Technology changes the form and competence of audit evidence,' *The CPA Journal*, 77 (1), pp. 68–70.

Duranti, L. (2010). 'The trustworthiness of digital records,' *InterPARES 3 Project: International Research on Permanent Authentic Records in Electronic System*. Available at: http://www.digitalrecordsforensics.org/

Duranti, L. and Blanchette, J. F. (2004). *The authenticity of electronic records: The InterPARES approach*. Available at: www.researchgate.net/publication/228612249_The_authenticity_of_electronic_records_the_InterPARES_ approach (Accessed 3 September 2021).

Duranti, L. and Jansen, A. (2011). *Authenticity of digital records: An archival diplomatics framework for digital forensics*. Available at: www.researchgate.net/publication/290042000_Authenticity_of_digital_records_An_archival_diplomatics_framework_for_digital_forensics (Accessed 3 September 2021).

Duranti, L. and Rogers, C. (2012). 'Trust in digital records: An increasingly cloudy legal area,' *Computer Law and Security Review*, 28, pp. 522–531.

Erima, A. J. and Wamukoya, J. (2012). 'Aligning records management and risk management with business processes: A case study of Moi University in Kenya,' *Journal of the South African Society of Archivists*, 45, pp. 24–38.

Hurbungs, V., Bassoo, V. and Fowdur, T. P. (2021). 'Fog and edge computing: Concepts, tools and focus areas,' *International Journal of Information Technology*, 1–15.

Information Regulator South Africa. (2020). *The media statement of the information regulator on the Experian security breach.* Available at: www.justice.gov.za/inforeg/docs/ms/ms-20200820-Experian.pdf (Accessed 10 September 2021).

InterPARES. (2002). *Requirements for assessing and maintaining the authenticity of electronic records.* Available at: www.interpares.org/book/interpares_book_k_app02.pdf (Accessed 3 September 2021).

INTOSAI Capacity Building Committee. (2020). *The future-relevant, value-adding auditor.* Available at: www.intosaicbc.org/wp-content/uploads/2020/11/20201106-The-Future-Relevant-Value-Adding-Auditor_CBC_Nov-2020.pdf (Accessed 12 September 2021).

ISA 500. (2009). *International Standards on auditing: audit evidence.* Available at: "https://www.ifac.org/system/files/downloads/a022-2010-iaasb-handbook-isa-500.pdf" Microsoft Word – A022 2010 IAASB Handbook ISA 500 (ifac.org) (Accessed 6 April 2022).

KPMG. (2020). *Remote auditing for internal auditors: Adjusting to the new normal.* Available at: https://assets.kpmg/content/dam/kpmg/be/pdf/2020/05/KPMG-Remote Auditing InternalAuditors.pdf (Accessed 1 June 2021).

Ma, J., Abie, H., Skramstad, T. and Nygard, M. (2009). *Requirements for evidential value for the assessment of the trustworthiness of digital records over time.* IEEE, pp. 1–8. Available at: file:///C:/Users/ngoepms/Downloads/Requirements_for_evidential_value_for_the_assessme.pdf (Accessed 21 September 2021).

Mentz, M., Barac, K. and Odendaal, E. (2018). 'An audit evidence planning model for the public sector,' *Journal of Economic and Financial Sciences*, pp. 1–14.

Mosweu, O. (2011). 'Performance audit in the Botswana public service and arising records management issues,' *Journal of the South African Society of Archivists*, 44, pp. 107–115.

Mosweu, O. (2018). *A framework to authenticate records in a government accounting system in Botswana to support the auditing process.* University of South Africa, Pretoria. PhD thesis.

Mosweu, O. and Ngoepe, M. (2021). 'Trustworthiness of digital records in government accounting system to support the audit process in Botswana,' *Records Management Journal*, 31 (1), pp. 89–108.

National Archives and Records Administration. (2005). *NARA guidance on managing web records.* Available at: www.archives.gov/records-mgmt/policy/managing-web-records.html (Accessed 12 June 2021).

National Archives and Records Services South Africa. (2006). *Managing electronic records in governmental bodies: Metadata requirements.* Available at: www.national.archives.gov.za/rms/NARS_DMLIB-4915-v1-NARS_DMLIB-Managing_electronic_records_metadata_requirements.PDF (Accessed 10 September 2021).

National Standard of Canada. (2017). *Electronic records as documentary evidence.* Ottawa: Canadian General Standards Board.

National Treasury. (2021). *National treasury: Integrated financial management system. Republic of South Africa.* Available at: www.ifms.gov.za/About.aspx#Background (Accessed 5 April 2021).

Nearon, B. H. (2005). 'Foundation in auditing and digital evidence,' *The CPA Journal*, 75 (1), p. 32.

Ngoepe, M.S. (2012). *Fostering a framework to embed the records management function into the auditing process in the South Africa public sector.* PhD Thesis, University of South Africa, Pretoria. Available at: https://uir.unisa.ac.za/handle/10500/15418 (Accessed 6 April 2022).

Ngoepe, M. and Mukwevho, J. (2018). *Ensuring authenticity and reliability of digital records to support the audit process (AF06).* InterPARES Trust Project. Available at: https://interparestrust.org/assets/public/dissemination/AF06-FinalReport.pdf (Accessed 19 January 2020).

Ngoepe, M. and Ngulube, P. (2014). 'The need for records management in the auditing process in the public sector in South Africa,' *African Journal of Library, Archives and Information Science*, 24 (2), pp. 135–150.

Nissen, T. (2018). *Technologies driving remote auditing.* Available at: www.cpapracticeadvisor.com/accounting-audit/news/12395206/technologies-driving-remote-auditing (Accessed 27 May 2021).

Omonuk, J. B. (2015). 'Computer assisted audit techniques and audit quality in developing countries: Evidence from Nigeria,' *Journal of Internet Banking and Commerce*, 20 (3), pp. 1–17.

Organisation for Economic Co-operation and Development. (2004). *Record-keeping guidance.* Available at: www.oecd.org/ctp/administration/31663114.pdf (Accessed 26 January 20202).

Pearce-Moses, R. (2005). *A glossary of archival and records terminology.* Chicago: The Society of American Archivists.

Pearce-Moses, R. (2019). 'Appendix 1: InterPARES trust terminology,' in L. Duranti and C. Rogers (eds.). *Trusting records in cloud.* Chicago: Facet.

Shneyder, D. (2020). *Voices auditing goes remote.* Available at: www.accountingtoday.com/opinion/auditing-goes-remote (Accessed 28 May 2021).

South African Law Reform Commission. (2019). *South African law reform commission report: Project 126.* Review of the law of evidence. Available at: www.justice.gov.za/salrc/reports/r_pr126ReviewoftheLawofEvidence2019.pdf (Accessed 19 July 2020).

South African National Standard 15801. (2013). *Document management – information stored electronically – recommendations for trustworthiness and reliability.* SABS Standards Division: South African Bureau of Standards. Pretoria.

Stancic, H., Ngoepe, M. and Mukwevho, J. (2019). 'Authentication,' in L. Duranti and C. Rogers (eds.). *Trusting records in cloud.* Chicago: Facet.

Teeter, R. A., Alles, M. G. and Vasarhelyi, M. A. (2010). 'The remote audit,' *Journal of Emerging Technologies in Accounting*, 7, pp. 73–88.

4 Trust dimensions of e-records in an African context

Beyond statutory provisions

Trywell Kalusopa and Tshepho Mosweu

Introduction

The management of digital records presents unique challenges in terms of their credibility as sources of information and evidence. To fulfil this trustworthy function, records must be managed in such a way that they remain complete, authentic, retrievable, and usable (Horsman, 2011). The concept of trust has been fundamentally advanced in the literature as the most important characteristic of digital organizations that deliver documents and records of lasting value to stakeholders (Donaldson and Conway, 2015). While the concept of trustworthiness is becoming increasingly important in the domain of managing digital sources, it appears to be understudied in the African context. This chapter attempts to provide a sketch narrative of its application in Africa based on empirical case studies of digital records management in enterprise-wide systems in the public sector in four countries: Botswana, Kenya, South Africa, and Zimbabwe. The chapter provides evidence, lays the groundwork for future understanding of enterprise architecture and its impact on digital records management, as well as the integration of ARM practice in digital and open government, and provides lessons to other African countries.

Trustworthy record: more than authentic record reliability

For any form of record to be considered authoritative evidence of business transactions, they should be considered trustworthy. Duranti and Rogers (2019) posit that trust involves acting without the knowledge needed to act. They agree that it consists of substituting the information that one does not have with other information, and that the "rules of trust refer to those who give trust as well as to those who receive trust: trustees [givers] and trustees [receivers]." In their persuasive submission, they contend that the trust

DOI: 10.4324/9781003203155-5

bond between trustees and trustees is usually based on four characteristics of the trustees. In that regard, the trustworthiness of a record as a statement of fact is based on the competence of its author, its completeness, and the controls on its creation. According to Duranti and Rogers (2019), this can be expressed in terms of accuracy, which is the correctness and precision of a record's content, based on the previous description, and the controls over content recording and transmission. It should also be grounded in authenticity whereby the trustworthiness of a record means that the record is what it purports to be, untampered with and uncorrupted, based on its identity and integrity, and on the reliability of the records system in which it resides.

A record that has trustworthiness is complete and unaltered (ISO 15489, 2016). To protect the integrity of digital records, policies and procedures should specify what additions or annotations are permissible after a record is created, under what circumstances, and who is authorized to make them (Franks, 2010). The International Council on Archives (ICA) (2016, p. 13) enunciates that, as records are products of work processes, it follows that the quality and trustworthiness of records depend on the quality and trustworthiness of the work processes that generate them, which means that if the work processes are poorly defined or inconsistent or not followed correctly, the records produced may not be adequate.

The use of diplomatics to assess the authenticity of a variety of documentary forms led to applying diplomatic principles in the digital environment and the development of a specialized field of "digital diplomatics" developed at the University of British Columbia (UBC) through the International Research on Permanent Authentic Records in Electronic Systems (InterPARES) research projects (Rogers, 2015, p. 7). To ensure the authenticity of digital records, practices should be in place to trace authorized annotation, addition to or deletion of a record, and that these should be explicitly indicated and traceable (Franks, 2010, p. 28). The International Organization for Standardization (ISO)15489–1 (2016) states that a record, regardless of form or structure, should possess the characteristics of authenticity, reliability, integrity, and usability to be considered authoritative evidence of business events or transactions and to fully meet the requirements of the business.

The integrity of records refers to record qualities as being reliable, authentic, and accessible in that they are whole and without corruption (International Council on Archives, 2016). As clearly stated by the Association of Records Managers and Administrators (ARMA), the principle of integrity requires that the information generated by or managed for an organization should have a reasonable and suitable guarantee of authenticity and reliability (ARMA, 2017). According to Duranti (2014), a document has integrity if the message communicates what it is supposed to communicate to ensure that its purpose is not altered, and for that to happen, the following integrity metadata must exist:

- name of handling persons over time;
- name of person responsible for keeping the record;
- indication of annotations;
- indication of technical changes;
- indication of presence or removal of a digital signature;
- time of planned removal from the system;
- time of transfer to a custodian; and
- time of planned deletion.

Trust in the Africa context: trends from selected countries

Most African countries have seen changes from manual record-keeping practices to digital ones as part of the e-government drive and transition in the public sector, where records may be supported by information and communication technologies (ICTs) or generated within ICT systems. Digital records generated within and managed by enterprise content management (ECM) systems raise issues of trustworthiness, that is, the authenticity and reliability of records. ARMA (2017) states that to ensure the integrity of information, the information assets generated by or managed for the organization need to have a reasonable guarantee of authenticity and reliability. In the digital environment, authenticity is an integral value that must be protected over time and across technological changes (Rogers, 2015, p. 2). Case studies done in Botswana, Kenya, South Africa, and Zimbabwe established the need for records management systems that ensure trustworthy records to support an open and e-government drive.

In Botswana, the Electronic Records (Evidence) Act (No. 13 of 2014) and the Electronic Communications and Transactions Act (No. 14 of 2014) work in tandem to ensure the legal admissibility and authenticity of electronic records and to facilitate electronic transactions. "Nothing in the rules of evidence shall apply to deny the admissibility of an electronic record in evidence on the sole ground that it is an electronic record" (Electronic Records (Evidence) Act, 2014, Section 5(1)). Furthermore, the Electronic Records (Evidence) Act states that "evidence may be presented in respect of any standard, procedure, usage, or practice concerning the matter in which the electronic records are to be recorded or stored" (No. 13 of 2014, Section 10), opening the door for consideration of electronic recordkeeping standards. The Electronic Communications and Transactions Act gives legal recognition to electronic communications outside the confines of evidence law. "Subject to the provisions of this Act, information shall not be denied legal effect, validity, or enforcement solely on the grounds that (a) it is in the form of an electronic communication" (No. 14 of 2014, Section 3). The Act states that electronic writing is sufficient to meet a legal requirement to give information in writing (Section 4). The Act also provides that the retention of electronic records is sufficient to meet legal retention obligations (Section 9), and that secure electronic signatures are sufficient for notarization and/or verification requirements (Section 11). When read in the context of these two Acts, one can discern **that** even if archival legislation does not expressly provide for a framework for the authorized use of electronic records.

According to a literature review conducted by Kalusopa et al. (2018), despite some weaknesses such as legislative, staffing, and organizational policy and practice issues, Botswana has a good ICT infrastructure, which is characterized by widespread use of ICT in the public service and progressive plans for improvement. A number of these ICTs constitute enterprise-wide systems and potential. The Association for Intelligent Information Management (AIIM) defines ECM as strategies, methods, and tools for capturing, managing, storing, preserving, and delivering content and documents related to organizational processes. ECM tools and strategies enable the management of an organization's unstructured information, regardless of where it exists (AIIM, 2010). ECM systems manage all types of relevant information for an organization, including records. ECM systems may or may not include a recordkeeping component, and they may or may not require intervention to identify and capture records. Enterprise-wide systems are similar to ECM applications but may lack some functions. Legislation, policy, and staffing issues complicate Botswana's enterprise-wide system and ECM implementations, but there is still a solid foundation from which to build a public service that manages digital records efficiently and effectively. Cloud computing is frequently used in enterprise-wide systems and ECM implementations. This review did not provide enough information to determine whether any of the systems or ECM implementations described were hosted in the cloud.

Among other examples, the most important enterprise-wide system in the Botswana public service is the Government Data Network (GDN). The Government of Botswana describes the GDN as the "basic technology platform for the rollout of e-Government services" (Botswana Government, 2011, p. 8). Most important for records management is the implementation of a National Archives and Records Management System (NARMS) by the Department of Botswana National Archives and Records Services (BNARS). Botswana's e-government strategy describes the purpose of this programme as "to provide on-line management of all government information" (Botswana Government, 2011, p. 15). Moatlhodi (2015) provides further context by noting that this application is an Electronic Document and Records Management System (EDRMS) based on the off-the-shelf HP Tower Records Information Management Context (TRIM) service (Moatlhodi, 2015, p. 4). Another important set of enterprise-wide systems comprises the various systems that Botswana has implemented to try to manage its lands. An International Records Management Trust (2008) case study notes four electronic land-management information systems: the Land Inventory for Tribal Land Boards of Botswana (LYNSIS), a Botswana Land Integrated System (BLIS), and a State Land Information Management System (SLIMS) with a parallel Tribal Land Information Management System (TLIMS) (IRMT, 2008, p. 10). All have attempted to address various aspects of land information management. At the time of the International Records Management Trust (IRMT) report, SLIMS and TLIMS were current. The Department of Tertiary Education Financing has a Student Loan Management System (Mosweu et al., 2014, p. 242). Not much more information was available. Botswana's Ministry of Trade and Industry has an EDRMS known as the Document Management Workflow System (DWMS) (Moatlhodi, 2015, p. 72; Mosweu et al., 2014). Mosweu (2012) notes that Botswana's Department of the Administration of Justice (AOJ) has a Court Records Management System (CRMS). The Maitlamo ICT policy document briefly describes a Police Private Network (Mosweu, 2012, p. 4). Its juxtaposition with the GDN would suggest that they are related in some way. Botswana's E-Government Strategy (2011) document also presents a multitude of other potential enterprise-wide systems and a complex diagram showing a variety of systems and their proposed linkages (Mosweu, 2012, pp. 15, 17).

In South Africa, the legislative framework promotes trust in the management of digital records. Thus, for example, the purpose of the Electronic Communications and Transactions Act (No. 25 of 2002) is to "enable and facilitate electronic communications and transactions," as well as to bring a greater degree of legal certainty to e-commerce and many areas that electronic communications touch. The most important parts of this Act from a records management perspective are the definitions (which provide a terminological framework for most subsequent Acts dealing with electronic records and information), and the definition of an original record vis-à-vis electronic record:

> Section 14(1) of the South African Electronic Communications and Transactions Act (No. 25 of 2002) requires information to be presented or retained in its original form, which requirement is met by a data message if –
>
> (a) the integrity of the information from the time it was first generated in its final form as a data message or otherwise has passed assessment in terms of subsection (2); and

(b) that information is capable of being displayed or produced to the person to whom it is to be presented.

(2) For the purposes of subsection 1(a), the integrity must be assessed –

(a) by considering whether the information has remained complete and unaltered, except for the addition of any endorsement and any change which arises in the normal course of communication, storage and display;
(b) in the light of the purpose for which the information was generated; and
(c) having regard to all other relevant circumstances.

Empirical evidence by Ngoepe and Katuu (2018) found that electronic public records and their proper management were a reality for all public sector institutions in South Africa. South Africa's laudable attempts to legislate and regulate digital records are not without shortcomings. In their highly relevant article *Managing digital records in a South African public sector institution*, Katuu and Ngoepe (2015) identify the major issue in South African public records as being able to distinguish an electronic original from an electronic copy. They advocate for a review of the definition of data management, arguing that record originals necessitate metadata as well as an electronic recordkeeping system. Properly defining records in evidentiary law, particularly electronic records, could help the effort to advance recordkeeping practices. The authors then draw a particularly pertinent analogy between information archaeology and information architecture. Information archaeology describes how old systems survive, and even sink and fade away beneath the new ones that are built on top of them. If government institutions are to properly manage records from the past, present, and future, they must acknowledge and provide for previous information systems. In South Africa, for example, national health institution information systems are highly fragmented and urgently require integration within each province before a nationwide plan can be implemented. This would necessitate the management of digital records originating not only from ECM but also from other systems (Katuu and Ngoepe, 2015). Having a specific storage mechanism in place is the last fundamental aspect of proper electronic records management. However, Katuu and Ngoepe (2015) found that no such electronic records storage system is in place.

Understanding the maturity levels of various ECM systems is a challenge in and of itself – one that will require additional research to fully conceptualize (Katuu, 2016). Findings show that organizational culture, change management, and the benefits and drawbacks of building systems on international standards are all factors in implementing any ECM model (Katuu, 2016), and they should be kept at the forefront of considerations in the future development of legislation and regulations.

A legal analysis in Zimbabwe also supports this. In that regard, the National Archives of Zimbabwe Act (1986) (Chapter 25:06) provides "for the storage and preservation of public archives and public records" (Section 3). Public archives are defined as:

(a) Any public record which –
   i. Is twenty-five years old; and
   ii. Has been specified by the Director as being of enduring or historical value; or

(b) Any other record or material acquired for the National Archives by the Director.

(Section 2).

Public records, in turn, are defined solely based on custody: " 'public record' means any record in the custody of any Ministry" (Section 2). Thus, records covered by the National Archives of Zimbabwe include, but are not limited to, public records. In particular, the director "may acquire by purchase, donation, bequest or otherwise any record or other material which in his/her opinion is or is likely to be of enduring or historical value" (Section 5(c)). Although the director has seemingly broad powers – he/she "may, in respect of any Ministry . . . inspect and examine [their] records [and/or] give advice or instructions concerning the filing, maintenance and preservation . . . of [those] records" (Section 6) – the director is ultimately limited by the discretion of the minister responsible for the said ministry, whose decision is final. Similarly, in cases where the director of the National Archives is denied access to records by a local authority, his/her only recourse is taking the issue to the relevant minister, who has the ultimate authority to grant or deny such access as s/he/they deem(s) fit. The role of the National Archives of Zimbabwe is largely circumscribed to an advisory role.

Understandably, given the colonial history of Zimbabwe, much of the National Archives Act is concerned with the protection of historical records, and the imposition of penalties upon individuals who would take such records. In the context of broader archival practice, however, the National Archives of Zimbabwe (NAZ) Act is both out of date and stingy in its context and guidance. The Act defines a "record" broadly enough that electronic records are almost certainly within its purview ("any medium in or on which information is recorded" [Section 2]); however, extraordinarily little guidance is given in the Act itself or secondary legislation as to what is to be done with and to those records and by whom. As Ngoepe and Saurombe (2016, p. 37), citing Mutsagondo and Chaterera (2016), put it, "Zimbabwe does not have archival legislation that specifically caters for the creation, use, maintenance and disposal of electronic records, which has resulted in records management practitioners resorting to a hit-or-miss approach when managing electronic records." Mutsagondo and Chaterera's (2016) survey of records managers working under the Act revealed that such critical areas as records transfer, destruction, authenticity, capacity, and an appraisal are all negatively impacted by the lack of legal guidance concerning electronic records. The Act also lacks provisions commonly found in archival laws, such as those providing for the legal authenticity of certified copies of records provided by the archives (be they paper or electronic). While the Act is broad and flexible and, therefore, could be updated through secondary legislation, no attempt has been made to do so thus far. It is worth noting that the NAZ Act (1986) was last updated in 2001, but still, electronic records were not specifically catered for.

The findings of a literature review by Chaterera et al. (2018) on enterprise digital records management in Zimbabwe show that some ECM modules may exist in Zimbabwe's public sector institutions, in particular, the ECM components for document management and records management. They may, however, appear under different headings and remain largely limited in the literature. Numerous institutions (particularly those in the public sector) such as museums and medical institutions continue to rely on manual systems, and many choose to ignore electronic mediums entirely due to financial constraints. The study also discovered that identifying ECM systems was difficult due to multiple definitions, as it is a relatively new field of study. Even if ECM systems were prevalent in Zimbabwe's public sector, they would not necessarily be declared or named explicitly. Nonetheless, the review identified the following public sector institutions as having the potential to implement ECM modules: the Ministry of Transport, Communication and Infrastructural Development, the Postal and Telecommunications Regulatory Authority of Zimbabwe (PORTRAZ), the Ministry of Science and Technology Development (MSTD), the Ministry of Finance, the Government Internet Service Provider (GISP), the Government Telecommunications Agency (GTA), and the Zimbabwe Academic and Research Network. Inadequacies in ICT policy and archival legislation amendments limit human resources and sporadic education and training, economic instability, and a lack of guidance from the archival community greatly hampers these initiatives.

In Kenya, the Access to Information Act (No. 31 of 2016) is meant to fulfil a number of accountability and transparency goals by providing access to records and other forms of information. The legislative purpose of the Access to Information Act is to:

(a) give effect to the right of access to information by citizens as provided under Article 35 of the Constitution;
(b) provide a framework for public entities and private bodies to proactively disclose information that they hold and to provide information on request in line with the constitutional principles;
(c) provide a framework to facilitate access to information held by private bodies in compliance with any right protected by the Constitution and any other law;
(d) promote routine and systematic information disclosure by public entities and private bodies on constitutional principles relating to accountability, transparency and public participation and access to information;
(e) provide for the protection of persons who disclose information of public interest in good faith; and
(f) provide a framework to facilitate public education on the right to access information under this Act.

(Access to Information Act, 2016, Section 3)

In addition to the duty to fulfil information requests, the Access to Information Act imposes several duties upon records professions in public entities. Article 17 provides for the "management of records," which are defined as "documents or other sources of information compiled, recorded or stored in written form or in any other manner and includes electronic records." Section 17(2) requires that public entities:

keep and maintain –

(a) records that are accurate, authentic, have integrity and useable; and
(b) its records in a manner which facilitates the right of access to information as provided for in this Act.

Section 17(3) imposes a duty to document and a requirement to digitize public entities.

The duty to document requires that public entities, at a minimum, "create and preserve such records as are necessary to document adequately [the entity's] policies, decisions, procedures, transactions and other activities it undertakes pertinent to the implementation of its mandate" (Section 17(3) (a)). The digitization requirement demands that, "not later than three years from the date from which this Act begins to apply to [a public entity, the entity shall] computerize its records and information management systems" (Section 17(3)(c)).

Moseti et al. (2018) established that ECM systems existed in the Kenyan public service. They generally form part of a concerted effort by public sector institutions to become more responsive to the people they serve. The Kenyan judiciary is in a position where it could integrate or may have already integrated enterprise-wide systems with records management functions. In other Kenyan public services, the connection between existing enterprise-wide systems and records management (RM) is tenuous. In all the cases, many of the problems identified by previous authors and within this paper – namely staffing, poor ICT implementations, decentralization, and poor policy and legislation – hamper records management functions. Broadly, the reality reflects Mnjama's (2003, p. 98) argument that, although digital records are included in the Kenya Public Archives and Documentation Service Act, Kenya has not moved to "establish how records created electronically are being managed." This accounts for the patchy nature of Kenya's enterprise-wide systems and their integration with Kenya's archives and records management. It is difficult to discern at this moment if there is any improvement in integration between enterprise-wide systems and archives and records management (ARM) within the identified organizations. However, the keen awareness of current problems in the professional literature, coupled with the recent willingness of the Kenyan government to address poor recordkeeping issues, suggests ample opportunity to make solid improvements. This provides some hope that future enterprise-wide system implementations will have a stronger connection to ARM. For Kenya, much work remains, but there are clear steps the country should take. For Kenyan ECM systems to be successful, they must be supported by improvements in the areas of infrastructure, policy, and training. Most importantly, Kenyan ECM applications must be integrated with ARM and should be built taking ARM into consideration.

Conclusion

Based on selected empirical studies presented in this chapter, it is instructive to assert that the trust dimension in managing digital records on the African continent is alive and evolving. Evidence obtained through literature review, legal analysis, and surveys contextualizes this in the implementation of enterprise-wide systems and ECM applications and the emerging cloud-based computing environment across Botswana, South Africa, Kenya, and Zimbabwe. However, despite this effort and policy motivations towards digital government initiatives, their connections to ARM practice are not well-grounded and require attention. The chapter draws on the recommendations for the need to exploit respective governments' apparent willingness to put in place a legal and regulatory framework supported by public sector reforms and initiatives as a basis to embed records and information management systems that would ensure the trustworthiness of digital records. While these studies do not cover the entire continent, they do provide evidence and lay the groundwork for understanding enterprise architecture and its impact on digital record management, as well as the integration of ARM practice in digital government in other African countries. As a result, the chapter's recommendations emphasize the need for a comprehensive legislative and policy framework, robust integration of ARM practice in government e-government efforts, and adequate technological infrastructure support.

References

Association for Intelligent Information Management (AIIM). (2010). *What is enterprise content management?* Available at: www.aiim.org/What – is – ECM – Enterprise – Content – Management.aspx (Accessed 13 July 2021).

Association of Records Managers and Administrators (ARMA). (2017). *Generally accepted recordkeeping principles.* Available at: www.arma.org/principles (Accessed 20 July 2021).

Botswana Government. (2011). *E-government strategy.* Available at: www.gov.bw/Global/Portal%20Team/1Gov_Strategy_Doc_2013.pdf (Accessed 26 January 2020).

Chaterera, F., Masuku, M., Bhebhe, S., Ngoepe, M. and Katuu, S. (2018). *Enterprise digital records management in Zimbabwe.* Available at: https://interparestrust.org/assets/public/dissemination/AF03ZimbabweLitReviewJuly2018.pdf (Accessed 20 July 2021).

Donaldson, D. R. and Conway, P. (2015). 'User conceptions of trustworthiness for digital archival documents,' *Journal of the Association for Information Science and Technology*, 66 (12), pp. 2427–2444.

Duranti, L. (2014). *Involuntary secondary permanence: Do many copies replace the one original.* Available at: https://interparestrust.org/assets/public/dissemination/Duranti_2014_YaleLibraries.pdf (Accessed 20 July 2021).

Duranti, L. and Rogers, C. (2019). *Trusting records and data in the cloud: The creation, management, and preservation of trustworthy digital content.* Available at: www.researchgate.net/publication/337398175 (Accessed 20 July 2021).

Franks, P. (2010). *How federal agencies can effectively manage records created using new social media tools.* Available at: www.businessofgovernment.org/report/how-federal-agencies-can-effectively-manage-records-created-using-new-social-media-tools (Accessed 20 July 2021).

Horsman, P. (2011). *Electronic record keeping: The record keeping system as framework for the management of electronic records.* Available at: www.archiefschool.n/docs/horselec.pdf (Accessed 20 July 2021).

International Council on Archives. (2016). *Managing metadata to protect the integrity of records.* Available at: www.ica.org/sites/default/files/Metadata%20Module.pdf (Accessed 1 June 2021).

International Organization for Standardization. (2016). *Information and documentation: Records management*. ISO 15489–1. Available at: www.iso.org/standard/62542.html (Accessed 20 January 2021).

International Records Management Trust (IRMT). (2008). *Fostering trust and transparency in governance: Botswana case study*. London: International Records Management Trust. Available at: www.irmt.org/documents/building_integrity/case_studies/IRMT_Case_Study_Botswana.pdf (Accessed 2 May 2021).

Kalusopa, T., Mosweu, T., Bayane, S., Ngoepe, M. and Katuu, S. (2018). *Implementation of enterprise-wide systems to manage trustworthy digital records in Botswana's public sector*. Available at: https://interparestrust.org/assets/public/dissemination/AF04BotswanaLit ReviewJuly2018.pdf (Accessed 20 July 2021).

Katuu, S. (2016). 'Assessing the functionality of the enterprise content management maturity model,' *Records Management Journal*, 26 (2), pp. 218–238.

Katuu, S. and Ngoepe, M. (2015). *Managing digital records in a South African public sector institution*. Available at: https://doi.org/10.17234/INFUTURE.2015.16 (Accessed 2 May 2021).

Mnjama, N. (2003). 'Archives and records management in Kenya: Problems and prospects,' *Records Management Journal*, 13 (2), pp. 91–101.

Moatlhodi, T. M. (2015). *An assessment of e-records readiness at the Ministry of Labor and Home Affairs Headquarters in Botswana*. University of Botswana, Gaborone. Unpublished master's dissertation in archives and records management.

Moseti, I., Maseh, E., Ngoepe, M. and Katuu, S. (2018). *Enterprise digital records management in Kenya*. Available at: https://interparestrust.org/assets/public/dissemination/AF05FinalReportMarch2018.pdf (Accessed 20 July 2021).

Mosweu, O., Mutshewa, A. and Bwalya, K. J. (2014). 'Electronic Document and Records Management System (EDRMS) implementation in a developing world context: Case of Botswana,' in K. J. Bwalya, P. M. Sebina and K. H. Moahi (eds.). *Digital access and e-government: perspectives from developing and emerging countries*. Harrisburg, PA: IGI Global, pp. 235–252.

Mosweu, T. (2012). *Assessment of the court records management system in the delivery of justice at the Gaborone Magisterial District*. University of Botswana, Gaborone. Unpublished master's dissertation in archives and records management.

Mutsagondo, S. and Chaterera, F. (2016). 'Mirroring the national archives of Zimbabwe act in the context of electronic records: Lessons for ESARBICA member states,' *Information Development*, 32 (3), pp. 254–259.

Ngoepe, M. and Saurombe, A. (2016). 'Provisions for managing and preserving records created in networked environments in the archival legislative frameworks of selected member states of the Southern African Development Community,' *Archives and Manuscript*, 44 (1), pp. 24–41.

Ngoepe, M. and Katuu, S. (2018). *Managing records in networked environments – South Africa*. Available at: https://interp1arestrust.org/assets/public/dissemination/AF02Li (Accessed 20 July 2021).

Rogers, C. (2015). 'Diplomatics of born digital documents – considering documentary form in a digital environment,' *Records Management Journal*, 25, pp. 6–20.

5 Tapestry of the education and training landscape for archives and records management in Africa

Shadrack Katuu

Introduction

Archives and records management (ARM) education and training has been the subject of numerous discussions for several decades (Hoy, 2004). In common parlance, education is viewed as introducing a learner to the theory and principles underpinning the professional practice in a discipline. Training provides the learner with a new skill (Franks, 2013, p. 289). It is immediately apparent that education programmes are more elaborate and run over a longer period than training programmes. Nonetheless, over the course of becoming an ARM professional, both education and training are essential to develop independent, competent lifelong learners.

The trajectory of discussions on ARM education and training in Africa has included both the historical and socio-cultural challenges related to accountability, good governance, emerging technological innovation, and the quest to unshackle from legacy structures (Ngoepe and Saurombe, 2021). Over the last three decades, African scholars have conducted several studies, ranging from opinion pieces, conference and seminar presentations, graduate-level research studies, and peer-reviewed studies on the state of ARM education and training on the continent (Ngoepe and Katuu, 2017). The purpose of this chapter is to provide an overview of ARM education and the training landscape in Africa. The chapter draws from research work conducted in case study AF01, *Curriculum Alignments at Institutions of Higher Learning in Africa: Preparing Professionals to Manage Records Created in Network Environments*, by the African team of the InterPARES Trust Project. The case study resulted in several research products, namely a review of the existing literature, two tracer studies of respondents from the African continent on their education and training experiences, and an inventory of education and training institutions in 38 of the 54 countries in Africa (Katuu et al. 2018a, 2018b, 2018c). Considering the extensive nature of all the research products, the tracer studies and inventory are not included in this chapter.

At the outset, two issues are important to note. First, a discussion of ARM education and training should be understood against the backdrop of the effects that colonization had on the socio-cultural, political, and administrative structures of individual African countries and, by extension, the ARM professionals in those countries (Katuu, 2020b, pp. 276–278). The legacy of colonial and post-colonial recordkeeping left by colonial masters was quite poor (Tough, 2012). Second, for a continent as vast as Africa, there is often an overwhelming temptation for an unhealthy reductionist discussion characterized by a few blanket statements, providing a bland picture based on a stereotype. The problem with stereotypes "is not that they are untrue, but that they are incomplete. They make one story become the only story" (Adichie, 2009, p. 5). Therefore, whenever discussing education and training in African countries, it is essential to acknowledge their complex national and regional socio-political contexts (Katuu, 2015, p. 97). Failure to do so results in oversimplification and a tendency to speak of 54 countries that make up nearly a billion people as a single entity. For this reason, the chapter is intentionally supported by an extensive reference list to reflect the diversity of approaches that exist on the African continent. This will ensure that other scholars can explore numerous lines of inquiry related to the ARM profession.

The rest of this chapter is divided into several sections. The following section provides historical context with selected examples of national and regional efforts in African ARM education programmes. The subsequent section adopts the systems thinking approach to provide an outline on the policy framework, institutional processes, and stakeholders or actors who constitute the tapestry of ARM education and training on the African continent.

Historical context

The history of ARM education on the African content is intertwined with its colonial history. During Africa's colonial period, the responsibility for recordkeeping was taken by the colonial administrators who had poor or non-existent recordkeeping structures (Tough, 2009). Alexander and Pessek (1988, p. 121) state that "despite some good intentions, the officials responsible for records administration – governors, colonial secretaries, department heads (there were no full-time professional archivists as such) – by and large failed dismally to live up to their responsibilities." Therefore, it was not surprising that very few efforts were made to educate or train the indigenous peoples of the different countries. From the end of the 1950s and throughout the 1960s, as African countries gained independence from their colonial masters, there was a realization that the records that were initially managed by colonial administrators would have to be managed by citizens of the newly independent countries. This realization took place at the same time as instances where exiting colonial administrators would either destroy or move records if they considered them incriminating, a common phenomenon in oppressive regimes. Historically, there were three general types of interventions and knowledge transfer efforts at the beginning of the post-colonial period. In the first, ARM professionals from colonial powers provided short-term assistance to newly independent countries like Kenya, Nigeria, Tanganyika, and Zanzibar (Charman and Cook, 1967). The second offered scholarships and fellowships to African practitioners to build their capacity in either Western Europe or North America through funding by nations or inter-governmental organizations like The United Nations Educational, Scientific and Cultural Organization (UNESCO) (Rieger, 1972). The third type, which had an impact that lasted almost two decades, was initiated in the mid-1960s by the International Council on Archives (ICA) with the support of the Society of American Archivists and UNESCO. The institutions discussed setting up two regional archival training centres in Africa (Dakar, Senegal and Accra, Ghana) to serve Francophone and Anglophone countries. During the 1970s, two regional centres were set up in Senegal and Ghana, in 1971 and 1975 respectively, with funding obtained from the United Nations Development Programme (UNDP) and the respective countries (Evans, 1988). However, UNDP withdrew funds from both centres in the early 1980s. Neither country could fill the funding gap and the situation necessitated the development of national schools (Thurston, 1985).

From the early 1980s, UNESCO, which had been involved in the development of regional centres, encouraged countries to establish their own national schools to establish a national school to "serve their own needs within the framework of . . . international standards" (Thurston, 1985, p. 119). Khayundi (2011, p. 63) states that most records professionals "who practiced before mid-1980s either did not have any training or were trained overseas," arguably in programmes that were not tailored to the needs of African students. A recent survey of institutions in Africa revealed that over 60 ARM education and training programmes were offered across 16 of the 54 African countries, including pre-university (certificate and diploma), undergraduate, and post-graduate levels like a master's and/or doctoral (Katuu, 2015, p. 140–141). However, these do not include other training programmes found in the continent, including pre-appointment education, on-the-job introductory education and training, or post-appointment continuing education and training, which resulted in a lack of standardization across the profession (Katuu, 2015, p. 101).

Considering the complex historical and social-cultural differences in individual countries, the rest of this section provides an illustrative rather than comprehensive overview of 11 of the possible 54 countries on the continent, listed in alphabetic order. Additionally, for some of the countries with a significant number of educational institutions, only a few are chosen to illustrate the developments.

It is important to highlight at least two known exceptions to the national ARM education and training programmes found on the continent. First, the Institute of Development Management (IDM) was established in 1974 by the president of Botswana and the Kings of Lesotho and Eswatini. They would combine their meagre resources to offer in-service short-term human resources, particularly to their civil services departments (Institute of Development Management, 2021a). The nations of Botswana, Eswatini, and Lesotho each host at least one IDM campus. In Botswana, IDM began its ARM certificate qualification in 2000, its diploma qualification in 2009, and eventually its bachelor's programme in 2016. Currently, IDM offers the ARM certificate diploma and bachelor's qualifications at the Botswana campus and the ARM diploma and bachelor's qualifications at the Eswatini campus. There is no ARM course or qualification in Lesotho (Institute of Development Management, 2021b). Second, the Eastern and Southern African Management Institute (ESAMI), which is an intergovernmental regional institution established by ten governments in 1980, is located in Tanzania (Eastern and Southern African Management Institute, 2021). These governments include Eswatini, Kenya, Malawi, Mozambique, Namibia, Seychelles, Tanzania, Uganda, Zambia, and Zimbabwe. ESAMI offers ARM courses as part of its qualifications and trains middle and senior managers from the region to improve their performance (Eastern and Southern African Management Institute, 2021).

Botswana

Botswana developed ARM education programmes through the University of Botswana's Department of Library and Information Studies (DLIS), which was initially set up in 1979 to offer diploma-level education in librarianship (Jain and Jorosi, 2015, p. 2). The department introduced an ARM certificate in 1995, an ARM diploma in 1997, and an ARM master's qualification in 2004 (Jain and Jorosi, 2015, pp. 7–8). Currently, it offers certificate, diploma, bachelor's, and master's ARM qualifications and a doctoral qualification with ARM specialization (University of Botswana, 2021). As noted, the country hosts an IDM campus, which provides ARM courses and qualifications.

Eswatini

Eswatini does not have an independent and indigenous tertiary-level institution that offers ARM courses or qualifications, even though there are advocacy efforts for an open distance e-learning programme (Chisita and Tsabedze, 2021). However, ARM practitioners can enlist in education and training opportunities at the IDM campus hosted in the country, which offers ARM courses and qualifications. If they are public sector officials, they can undertake ARM courses at ESAMI in Tanzania.

Ghana

Ghana developed ARM education programmes at the University of Ghana, which hosted the Ghana Library School in 1961, moved to the institution in 1965, and was re-designated as the Department of Library Studies in 1965 (University of Ghana, 2021). In 1976, the department was renamed the Department of Library and Archival Studies when it started hosting the Centre for Archival Education in Anglophone Africa, offering a diploma and graduate diploma in ARM until its demise in 1982 (University of Ghana, 2021). Subsequently, it was renamed the Department of Information Studies and currently offers ARM courses as part of its information studies qualifications (University of Ghana, 2021).

Kenya

Kenya's earliest ARM education and training programme began in 1979 at the Kenya Polytechnic. During the 1980s and 1990s, the institution offered ARM qualifications at the certificate, diploma, and higher diploma levels. In 2013, the institution was converted to the Technical University of Kenya (TUK). Its Department of Information and Knowledge Management currently offers ARM certificate and diploma qualifications, as well as ARM courses within its other bachelor's and master's qualifications (Technical University of Kenya, 2021). Even though TUK's predecessor institution was the first to have ARM qualifications in 1979, there are over a dozen other institutions that currently offer ARM education and training opportunities. The rest of this section provides an illustrative sample of the institutions.

The Moi University's Faculty of Information Science, later known as the School of Information Science, was established in 1988. The Department of Library and Information Studies was established in 1989 and the Department of Archives and Records Management was established in 1991 (Katuu, 2009, p. 140). The school was the first in Kenya to offer an ARM qualification at the undergraduate level. During the 2005–2006 academic year, the school's two departments merged into the Department of Library, Records Management, and Information Studies. It continues to offer ARM qualification at the master's level and ARM specialization options at the bachelor's and doctoral levels (Moi University, 2021).

Other Kenyan universities that offer ARM courses and/or qualifications include:

- The Catholic University of East Africa's Department of Library and Information Science offers ARM qualifications at the certificate and diploma levels, as well as ARM courses in its bachelor's qualification.
- Kenya Methodist University's Department of Information Science offers an ARM qualification at the certificate level and ARM courses in its bachelor's and master's qualifications.
- Kenyatta University's Department of Library and Information Science used to offer ARM electives in its bachelor's and master's programmes in the 2000s. It currently offers ARM qualifications at the bachelor's and master's levels, and ARM specialization at the doctoral level (Katuu, 2009, p. 141).
- Kisii University's Department of Library and Information Science offers ARM courses in its bachelor's, master's, and doctoral qualifications.
- Mount Kenya University's Department of Information Science and Knowledge Management offers ARM qualifications at the certificate and diploma levels, as well as ARM courses in its bachelor's and master's qualifications.

Finally, as discussed earlier in this section, the government partly owns ESAMI; therefore, it can send its public sector officials to undertake ARM courses at the institution.

Lesotho

Lesotho does not have an independent and indigenous tertiary-level institution that offers ARM courses or qualifications. Even though it hosts an IDM campus, it does not offer ARM courses (Institute of Development Management, 2021b). Therefore, ARM practitioners must go outside the country to obtain education and training qualifications.

Malawi

In 2009, it was reported that Mzuzu University offered ARM courses in diploma and bachelor's programmes (Gondwe, 2020, p. 280). Since the 1990s, efforts have been made to offer fully fledged ARM diploma and degree programmes, at least at the University of Malawi and Mzuzu University; however, this has not materialized (Gondwe, 2020, p. 281). Instead, most professionals obtain their training from private firms within the country or through education and training opportunities outside the country (Gondwe, 2020, p. 290). Lastly, as mentioned, the government partly owns ESAMI and, therefore, can send its public sector officials to undertake ARM courses at the institution in Tanzania.

Namibia

In 1995, the University of Namibia's Department of Library and Information Studies introduced an information studies programme for graduate information professions, including diploma and bachelor's qualifications with an ARM specialization option (Nengomasha, 2006, p. 209). In 1997, it changed its name to the Department of Information and Communication Studies to reflect the broadening of its base in information studies courses (Nengomasha, 2006, p. 209). By 2008, the department was offering a diploma-level ARM qualification with ARM courses in other diploma and bachelor's programmes (Nengomasha, 2006, p. 209). Currently, the department offers diploma, bachelor's, master's, and doctoral ARM qualifications, as well as ARM courses for other qualifications (University of Namibia, 2021). Lastly, as mentioned, the government partly owns ESAMI and, therefore, can send its public sector officials to undertake ARM courses at the institution in Tanzania.

Nigeria

Nigeria's earliest library sciences education and training programme began as the Institute of Librarianship within the University Library in 1959 (University of Ibadan, 2021b). In 1965, it changed its name to the Department of Library Studies and then to the Department of Library, Archival, and Information Studies in the mid-1980s when it started offering ARM courses (University of Ibadan, 2021b). The department currently offers a master's qualification in ARM (University of Ibadan, 2021a).

Other Nigerian universities that offer ARM courses and/or qualifications include:

- Ahmadu Bello University's Department of Library and Information Science was established in 1968 (Ahmadu Bello University, 2021a). The department currently offers ARM courses in bachelor's and master's qualifications (Ahmadu Bello University, 2021b; Ahmadu Bello University, 2021c).
- Nnamdi Azikiwe University's Department of Library and Information Science offers ARM courses in bachelor's and master's qualifications (Nnamdi Azikiwe University, 2021).

Senegal

As noted, Senegal had one of the first two training centres in Africa, which was established in 1971. The programme was eventually incorporated into the School of Librarians, Archivists, and Documentalists at the Université Cheikh Anta Diop de Dakar. The school currently offers ARM specializations in bachelor's and master's qualifications (Université Cheikh Anta Diop de Dakar, 2021a; Université Cheikh Anta Diop de Dakar, 2021b).

South Africa

South Africa's history differs significantly from most other countries in sub-Saharan Africa for two reasons. First, the nation started ARM education and training discussions at the nation's archival institution in the late 1940s (Ngoepe, 2008). Staff working at the institution were considered professionals if they held a Bachelor of Arts (BA) degree concentrating on history and underwent in-house training. Harris (1996, pp. 7–10) notes that the country's Public Service Commission approved a curriculum in archival science in 1950, including an examination that one had to pass to be considered a professional. In 1965, a post-graduate national diploma in archival science administered by the Department of National Education was introduced with the prerequisite still being the BA with a focus on history (Harris, 1996, pp. 7–10). In the 1990s, the national diploma course was moved to Technikon South Africa and the contribution of the National Archival Institution diminished over time. By the late 1990s, the University of KwaZulu-Natal, as well as the University of Witwatersrand, offered programmes at honours, master's, and doctoral levels, as well as a post-graduate diploma (Ngoepe, 2008, p. 75).

The second feature is the radical restructuring of higher education institutions between 2000 and 2006, as well as how that impacted ARM education and training in the country (Department of Arts and Culture [South Africa] 2010). The restructuring saw 36 public institutions merged into 23. Consequently, the institutions reviewed their academic offerings, which resulted in the number of universities exclusively offering ARM qualifications being reduced from five in the early 2000s to three in the early 2010s (Department of Arts and Culture [South Africa] 2010, p. xxi). However, there are additional institutions that offer ARM courses in other programmes.

The University of South Africa (UNISA), which is the preeminent institution in ARM education and training in the country, introduced ARM courses in its information science qualifications in 2000 (Ngoepe, 2008, p. 76). During the restructuring process, it inherited the ARM qualifications offered at the former Technikon South Africa. It consolidated the resources and infrastructure within its Department of Information Science (Ngoepe,

2008, p. 76). The department currently offers ARM qualifications at higher certificate and bachelor's levels, honours, and the ARM specialization at master's and doctoral levels (University of South Africa, 2021b, 2021c). Other South African universities that offer ARM courses and/or qualifications include:

- The University of Fort Hare's Department of Library and Information Science has offered a post-graduate diploma in ARM qualification since 2007 (Department of Arts and Culture [South Africa] 2010, p. 114). Currently, the department offers an ARM qualification and ARM courses in its undergraduate and master's programmes.
- Since the 2000s, the University of Johannesburg's Department of Information and Knowledge Management offered an ARM module in its information management honour's degree.
- The University of KwaZulu-Natal's Department of Information Studies has offered an ARM post-graduate diploma since the 2000s. For a period, it suspended the diploma due to a lack of staff, but it was resumed in 2010 once the relevant staff member was appointed (Department of Arts and Culture [South Africa] 2010, p. 107). Currently, the department offers an ARM qualification at the post-graduate diploma level, as well as the ARM specialization in master's and doctoral qualifications.
- The University of Witwatersrand's School of Graduate Studies offered a post-graduate course in ARM in the 2000s (Department of Arts and Culture [South Africa] 2010, p. 107).
- Since the 2000s, the University of Zululand's Department of Information Studies has offered ARM courses in its undergraduate and diploma qualifications (Department of Arts and Culture [South Africa] 2010, p. 106).

Zimbabwe

Since the 1980s, Zimbabwe's earliest ARM education and training courses were at the Harare Polytechnic (Katuu, 2009, p. 141). The institution currently offers ARM qualifications at the certificate, diploma, and higher diploma levels. Other Zimbabwean universities that offer ARM courses and/or qualifications include:

- The National University of Science and Technology, which was established in 1991, began offering ARM qualifications in 2004 (Khumalo and Chigariro, 2017, p. 68). Currently, the institution's Department of Records and Archives Management offers ARM qualifications at the bachelor's and master's levels (National University of Science and Technology, 2021).

- Zimbabwe Open University's Department of Information Science and Records Management offers an ARM qualification at the bachelor's level (Zimbabwe Open University, 2021).

Lastly, as mentioned, the government partly owns ESAMI, which allows its public sector officials to undertake ARM courses at the institution in Tanzania.

Education system: a systems thinking approach

In most countries, formal ARM education and training programmes operate within an education system, specifically a higher education system. These systems are made up of a complex interaction of elements, including stakeholders or actors and assets (infrastructure and equipment) regulated by a policy framework to produce learning outcomes (Kaffenberger, 2021). Higher education systems comprise complex relationships that constitute disparate interactions among people, economies, government structures, laws, ethics, and cultural norms (Dhukaram et al., 2018). A discussion of ARM education and training systems in each African country would require detailed and highly nuanced elaboration. Therefore, it is necessary to use a systems approach to provide a meta-analysis of the elements constituting the disparate systems. Systems thinking is an approach that seeks to understand the connections among elements in a system. This section adopted a systems framework espoused by Dhukaram et al. (2018), which consists of a policy and regulatory context, organizational processes and procedures, and stakeholders.

Policy and regulatory context

One challenge for ARM educators relates to the introduction of ARM professionals to the complex web of the legislative, regulatory, and best practice framework within which ARM work is done. While ARM educators were building programmes from the 1980s into the 2000s, they had to contend with the rapid introduction of information management legal and regulatory norms across the globe. The most fundamental act in most countries would be the national records and/or archives act. Some nations, such as Kenya, had such legislation in 1965, two years after attaining independence from the British in 1963. In 1962, Uganda also gained independence; however, it only enacted its national archival legislation in 2001. For the most part, most African countries have national archival legislation.

A more disruptive legislative trend was the global movement for access to information, also known as the right to information or freedom of information legislation. The Organisation of African Unity (1981), the predecessor of the current African Union, recognized an individual's right to receive information in its African Charter on Human and People's Rights, Article 9. Since the 1980s, regional and international organizations applied both direct and indirect pressure on tenants of good governance and accountability in public sector reform initiatives globally. Other African examples include the Declaration of Principles on Freedom of Expression in Africa, the African Charter on Democracy, Elections, and Good Governance (African Union, 2007), and the Model Law on Access to Information for Africa (African Commission on Human and People's Rights, 2013). These efforts underpinned the passage of access to information legislation or constitutional provisions in a number of countries from the 1990s through the 2010s (Lemieux and Trapnell, 2016, p. 14).

There are two trends in the enactment of access to information legislation. First, some countries have enacted fully fledged legislation, often accompanied by implementation regulations. These include South Africa and Zimbabwe in 2002, Uganda in 2005, Liberia and Guinea in 2010, Nigeria in 2011, Cote d'Ivoire and Rwanda in 2013, Burkina Faso in 2015, and Kenya, Malawi, Tanzania, and Tunisia in 2016 (Right2Info, 2021). Second, some countries only have a constitutional provision. These include Mozambique in 1990, Ghana and Madagascar in 1992, Seychelles in 1993, Ethiopia in 1994, Guinea Bissau in 1996, Senegal in 2001, Angola in 2002, Democratic Republic of Congo in 2006, and Cape Verde in 2010 (Right2Info, 2021).

Global experiences have shown that access to information legislation has the potential to positively impact recordkeeping and provide an enormous opportunity for ARM professionals (Shepherd, 2012, p. 176). Similar trends could be laid out for other legislation with an impact on recordkeeping, including data protection or data privacy and protection of personal information.

Institutional processes and procedures

Certain institution-level priorities guide and foment the implementation of ARM education and training. This section outlines institutional processes and procedures that constitute such an education system.

Curriculum development

Curriculum is at the core of education provision. Considering the history of many ARM programmes in Africa, curricula were initially informed by practices in the global north due to the legacy of colonization and marginalization of African cultures like orality (Bhebhe and Ngoepe, 2021). There has been a movement to transform the curricula with three broad trends. In the first trend, individual institutions transform their curricula. Ngoepe et al. (2022) document the process used by the University of South Africa's

ARM education programme to revise its curriculum to align with international trends and practices in the management of digital records. The second trend involves two or more institutions that collaborate to develop curricula. There seems to be no immediate African example to share. An example from the Global North includes three institutions (Canada, the United Kingdom, and the United States of America [USA]) that have collaboratively worked on developing the concept of computational archival science (Marciano, Lemieux et al., 2019). Of the three institutions (Canada's University of British Columbia, the UK's King's College London, and the University of Maryland in the USA), the latter seems to have extensively mapped its curriculum to align with the computational archival science framework (Marciano, Agarrat et al., 2019). The third trend, and perhaps the most impactful, is where professional associations develop the ARM curriculum framework. From the 1980s to the mid-2010s, professional associations in Canada and the USA sought to develop an understanding of what constitutes professional curriculum by identifying core vs. complementary knowledge areas (Society of American Archivists, 2016).

Theory vs. practical training

One of the main issues noted in the delivery of ARM education is the balance of theory vs. practice. As noted, in common parlance, education is viewed as introducing a learner to the theory and principles underpinning the professional practice in a discipline. Training provides a learner with a new skill (Franks, 2013, p. 289). Historically, many of Africa's ARM education programmes had a tendency towards skill-building rather than the development of a professional mindset (Katuu, 2009, p. 136). For instance, in a debate on the nature of education at the University of South Africa, Theron (1998, p. 114) noted that education involved instilling the capacity to learn rather than training by drilling or transferring skills or specific techniques. A skill-building environment that, among other things, uses an educational model of rote memorization, tends to "view students as embryonic professionals rather than as academic creatures who primarily assimilate and analyze concepts and by extension are competent to determine the connections between theory and practice" (Katuu, 2009, p. 138). This trend is not unique to Africa. According to Jimerson (2010, p. 3), North American ARM education emphasized practical skill development over an integrated theoretical foundation through the mid-1980s. Eventually, growing numbers of archival educators resulted in an emphasis on archival theory rather than practical experience (Jimerson, 2010, p. 3).

There is a concern about an overly theoretical emphasis (Garaba, 2015, p. 217). Graduates from Uganda's Makerere University lamented that the theoretical curriculum did not provide them with important practical skills, requiring them to undergo lengthy in-service training before starting their new jobs (Lutwama and Kigongo-Bukenya, 2004, p. 106). For this reason, several programmes introduced experiential opportunities through internships, work studies, or similar programmes. These may differ in duration from several days to several weeks, either once or twice during the course of an ARM qualification, for instance, in Botswana, Ghana, Namibia, or Zimbabwe. The emphasis should be on providing a balance between theory and practice so graduates have both the conceptual and practical skill set needed to thrive in the field (Noko and Ngulube, 2015, p. 281). In addition, there must be a balance between theory and practice relevant to national and regional needs.

Embracing technology

From the 1990s through the 2010s, African scholars lamented the inadequate knowledge and training of educators in information and communication technologies within the profession (Garaba, 2015). The advent of government reform programmes of the 1990s and e-government transformation of the 2000s put additional impetus on professionals to assess and acquire appropriate technology competencies in their ARM education and training programmes (Nengomasha, 2006, p. 214).

Many technology trends are discussed in the context of the Fourth Industrial Revolution, a term attributed to Klaus Schwab. This industrial revolution follows the mechanization of the agrarian society, road and telecommunication infrastructure, and ubiquity of digital technologies in the first to third industrial revolutions, respectively. The fourth revolution is characterized by an increased use of smart technology, as well as the automation of traditional manufacturing and industrial practices (Katuu, 2021b, p. 62). The themes discussed in this context include cloud computing, blockchain technology, enterprise-wide systems, and architectural disciplines like enterprise and information architecture.

Cloud computing technology has its roots in the networking of computing infrastructures in the 1970s. Its most modern form emerged in the early 2000s and enables "ubiquitous, convenient, on-demand network access to a shared pool of configurable computing resources (e.g., networks, servers, storage, applications, and services) that can be rapidly provisioned and released with minimal management effort or service provider interaction" (Mell and Grance, 2011). Katuu (2021b, p. 63) argues that this technology brings both challenges and opportunities to ARM professionals in Africa. Cloud technologies have become the platform on which to host off-premises applications using thin-client architecture on mobile devices. This has evolved from on-premises applications that limited practitioner agility

(Katuu, 2021b, p. 63). Challenges included the loss of jurisdictional control over public records that are managed and stored in disparate locations outside a nation (Katuu and Ngoepe, 2015, p. 66).

Blockchain technology, which was first implemented in the late 2000s, is most widely known to support cryptocurrencies. Lemieux et al. (2019) consider it a technology of trust, describing it as a type of distributed ledger comprised of confirmed and validated blocks cryptographically chained together. The technology can be used as a recordkeeping system, even though there are shortcomings in the design, implementation, and governance for the technology to be considered as ideal for trustworthy public recordkeeping.

Institutions are increasingly implementing enterprise-wide systems like customer relationship management (CRM), supply chain management (SCM), and enterprise resource planning (ERP) systems, particularly in integrating disparate business processes in real time (Katuu, 2020a, 2021a). These systems tend to be expansive, integrating vast aspects of institutional processes and supporting thousands (sometimes hundreds of thousands) of transactions per minute. For this reason, the identification, capturing, and management of records generated in such systems would have to use digital means. To respond to this challenge, ARM education and training programmes could draw guidance from professional good practice; for instance, the ISO 16715 standard on processes and functional requirements for managing records provides guidance, stating there are at least three possible scenarios (International Standards Organization, 2020):

1) A business application has internal records management capabilities.
2) A business application has a records management application component as a separate specialized sub-system.
3) A business application uses records management services that are autonomous from a separate application.

Various versions of these scenarios have either been implemented or are being explored by ARM practitioners, including in Botswana, Kenya, South Africa, and Zimbabwe (Chaterera et al. 2018; Kalusopa et al., 2018; Katuu, 2018a; Mello, 2020; Moseti et al., 2018; Mosweu et al., 2019).

Organizations are increasingly using architecture disciplines, such as security or enterprise solutions, to assess information technology ecosystems and align any developments with institutional goals. For instance, enterprise architecture consists of a collection of special documents or artefacts that describe various aspects of an organization from an integrated perspective. This links the institutional mission, strategy, and processes to its information strategy (Katuu, 2019, p. 3116). Leveraging enterprise architectural principles makes it possible to embed recordkeeping in the strategic goals of an institution, and to influence systems analysis, design, planning, and change management (Katuu, 2018b). For this reason, the ISO 21965 standard on records management in enterprise architecture was developed to provide a common understanding for records professions and enterprise architects about requirements for records processes and systems (International Standards Organization, 2019). Enterprise architecture is relatively new to ARM practitioners; therefore, exploratory discussions and experiences have only started to emerge. Examples of such discussions include professionals in international organizations (Katuu, 2021c) and a doctoral study in a South African institution (Mello, 2020).

Engaging in research

Considering the discussion related to curriculum, the tension between theory and practice, and the topic of embracing technology, there is a need to incorporate research in ARM education and training activities. Shepherd (2012, p. 176) argues that there is a danger of losing the war to save the profession without the establishment of a research base. According to Schaeffer (1997, p. 73), graduate-level education is the best setting to develop "a compelling and coherent body of theory and to make education in this theory relevant" to the profession. Until the late 1990s, ARM professionals in Africa did not actively contribute to global research activities due to a lack of constant and prolonged exposure to such efforts (Ngoepe et al., 2014). For this reason, efforts have been made to improve ARM education, in general, and, particularly, in graduate education. For instance, between 2013 and 2019, the University of South Africa's Department of Information Science coordinated the activities of an African team of educators, practitioners, and graduated students as part of the InterPARES Trust research project (Katuu, 2016)).

ARM qualifications or ARM specializations in other courses

Beyond a discussion of the curriculum, the intricate balance between theory and practice, and the incorporation of technology, is the debate about the levels and types of ARM qualifications offered. First, with regard to levels, there are generally three major categories (Katuu, 2015, p. 7):

1 pre-university qualifications: certificate, higher certificate, diploma, and higher diploma qualifications;
2 undergraduate university qualifications: hues of first-degree qualifications; and
3 graduate (post-graduate)-level qualifications: post-graduate certificate, post-graduate diploma, and hues of master's degrees and doctoral degree qualifications.

In many cases, institutions determine the levels of ARM qualifications offered based on internal dynamics and national priorities.

Second, with regard to types, the many nuanced variations can be divided into independent and generic qualifications. An independent ARM qualification could be a certificate or degree that is explicitly identified as ARM. This includes all or most of the curriculum covering ARM courses. A generic qualification may be offered in a related discipline, such as information science or information studies, and have limited contribution of ARM courses in the curriculum. Based on a general assessment of ARM programmes, independent ARM qualifications tend to dominate at the pre-university level, with a possible equal measure of independent and generic qualifications at the undergraduate and graduate levels (Katuu et al., 2018a). Beyond these general trends, each institution within individual countries may have variations. For instance, in South Africa, the University of South Africa introduced an independent ARM qualification at the undergraduate level; however, it remains with specialization at the master's and doctoral levels (University of South Africa, 2021a).

Continuing Professional Development (CPD)

ARM education and training discussions would not be complete without the discussion of state CPD, which is the "systematic method of learning that leads to growth and improvement in professional abilities, enabling individuals to function successfully in a changing work environment" (Majid, 2004, p. 58). Competency-based training for CPD and involvement in research-based enquiry and knowledge creation are both needed to sustain well-rounded professionals (Anderson, 2007, p. 94). The purpose of CPD activities is to "fill the knowledge gaps between formal education and the needs of the professional practice" (Majid, 2004, p. 58). For instance, in 2006, the Swedish International Development Cooperation Agency's (SIDA) Records Management in Service of Democracy (RMSD) programme supported ARM professionals from southern and eastern Africa (Justrell, 2007). However, Anderson (2007, p. 98) argues that "an unstructured aggregation of short courses alone is unlikely to lead to the development of well-rounded professionals." Therefore, it is necessary to develop multiple paths of learning outcomes and strategies, namely competency-based learning, workplace learning, reflective learning, and self-directed learning (Hoy, 2004, pp. 13–15).

In Australia, two professional associations developed a guide to record-keeping for professionals. This guide included tasks, competencies, and expected salaries in six progressive bands of their professional careers (ASA and RMAA Joint Education Steering Committee, 2010). It follows a capability of maturity model with six levels, as well as indicators of the tasks for each level, academic certification, and descriptive information related to remuneration.

Stakeholders

A coherent education system includes several actors and/or stakeholders, such as teachers, students, administrators, and institutional actors (Dhukaram et al., 2018, pp. 11–13). This section discusses the contribution of five such stakeholders.

Policy or government stakeholders

Policy or government stakeholders are at the highest level of accountability in any education system. To fulfil the core purpose of an education system, there is a need for "strong political will and the commitment and dedication of leaders to explicit learning goals, and the clear communication and delegation of these goals to the rest of the system" (Kaffenberger, 2021). An issue of concern for policy makers in African universities has been the need to introduce a systematic national qualifications framework given the varied nature of qualifications offered in diverse institutions of higher learning. In South Africa, this process culminated in a higher education qualifications framework law in 2007. At the time of the introduction, there was concern that new titles (higher certificate, advanced certificate, and post-graduate diploma) would cause confusion. Figure 5.1 shows the current National Qualification Framework (NQF) levels and qualification types, as well as the responsible institutions.

Since its introduction in South Africa, there seems to have been more clarity regarding the ten NQF levels, the interaction between the four regulating institutions, and the equivalences between different qualifications. ARM education programmes in institutions like UNISA constantly refer to the framework in their communication (University of South Africa, 2021a).

In Kenya, a law enacted in 2014 established the Kenya National Qualifications Authority (KNQA) to help coordinate and harmonize the various levels of education in the country (Kenya National Qualifications Authority, 2021a). KNQA is developing "an accurate, reliable and robust database of all qualifications in the country that will allow for comparability, equation, recognition and information sharing of qualifications globally" (Kenya National Qualifications Authority, 2021a). Figure 5.2 shows the levels and qualification types:

The qualification framework is not as embedded in Kenyan education programmes as in South Africa due to legacy challenges and the introduction of

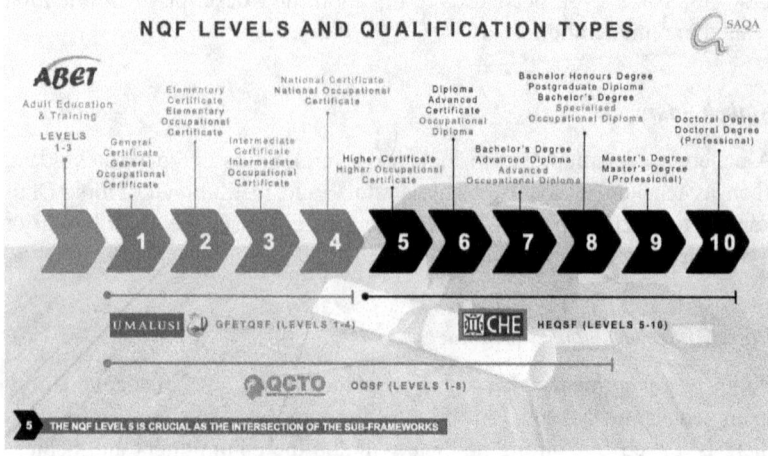

Figure 5.1 South Africa's National Qualification Framework levels and qualification types

Long description: Graph showing progression of South Africa's National Qualification Framework levels from Adult Education and Training on the left side progressing through several certificates, diploma, degree, masters and doctoral qualifications on the right side.

(*Source*: Department of higher education and training [South Africa] and South Africa Qualifications authority [2017])

a nationwide curriculum, starting in elementary school. Nonetheless, qualifications frameworks are a valuable step in determining equivalence within a country and between countries, supporting students between phases of learning, and bridging the gap between education and practice.

ARM educators

At the core of ARM education and training activities are the educators and trainers in varied institutions. For quality learning to take place, there is need for "research-based higher education, particularly at the doctoral level" because this is increasingly becoming the base qualification for appointment to teaching posts in university professional education programmes that function to supply qualified practitioners, future educators, as well as nature research projects that solve problems and build new knowledge (Anderson, 2007, p. 103). An example of research projects where African ARM educators have contributed were those developed by the International

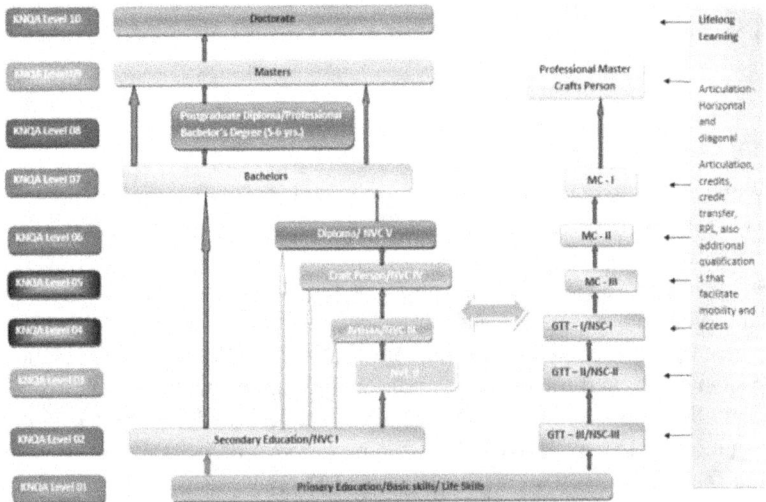

Figure 5.2 Kenya's National Qualification Framework levels and qualification types

Long description: Graph showing progression of Kenya's National Qualification Framework levels from primary education at the bottom in Level 1 through secondary education progressing through several certificates, diploma, degree, masters and doctoral qualifications at the top.

Source: Kenya National Qualifications authority, 2021b

Records Management Trust (IRMT), which was established in 1989, drawing from the experience of founder Dr. Anne Thurston, while working as an ARM educator at the University College London. Over the course of 30 years until it closed in 2019, the IRMT coordinated the development of educational material and tools and conducted research. This established a rich resource of free knowledge products on its website (Katuu, 2020b, pp. 280–281). During this time, the IRMT (2018) partnered with many African ARM educators to conduct consultancy projects in countries like Botswana, the Democratic Republic of the Congo, Egypt, Ethiopia, Ghana, Kenya, Lesotho, Nigeria, South Africa, Tanzania, The Gambia, Uganda, Zambia, and Zimbabwe.

Between 2013 and 2019, the University of South Africa's Department of Information Science coordinated the activities of an African team of educators, practitioners, and graduated students as part of the InterPARES Trust research project (Katuu, 2016). The book to which this chapter is a contribution is one of the many knowledge products generated by the African team of the project. ARM educators have continued to engage in these kinds of research and modern digital challenges like cloud computing (Katuu and Ngoepe, 2015).

ARM students

While educators form the supply side of knowledge, ARM students are seen as the receiving side of that knowledge. Many African institutions of higher learning have been plagued by poor learning methodologies. In these, learners were viewed as "embryonic professionals rather than as academic creatures who primarily assimilate and analyze concepts" (Katuu, 2009, p. 138).

Nonetheless, a major contribution of ARM students to the education system has been through tracer studies, which are empirical evaluations of institutional programmes. Only one of the studies, conducted by Noko and Ngulube (2015), exclusively collected data from ARM graduates. The reason for this is that the other institutions had graduates with more general qualifications in information science, library, and information studies.

Nonetheless, the studies were able to provide feedback, allowing educational institutions to validate the learning outcomes and employability patterns. In addition, they could understand emerging professional challenges and provide catalysts for curricula review and reform.

Educational institutions

Among the many challenges in educational institutions that offer the different types and levels of ARM education, are a low number of qualified staff, poor quality of educational materials, and obsolete programmes. However, these institutions also contribute to the challenges in two ways. First, they have varied interpretations of macro-decisions made by national policy stakeholders. Second, they make decisions via the institutional leadership. In the first instance, for example, when South African national policymakers decided to restructure universities in the 2000s, resulting in a reduction from 36 to 24 universities and later to 26, some individual universities hosting ARM programmes also decided to abolish those programmes, reducing the offerings in the country from five to three (Katuu and Ngoepe, 2017, p. 22). An example of the second instance relates to the placement of ARM programmes within institutions. In the past, ARM education programmes were associated with history or library programmes. However, the global trend is increasingly for programmes to be located in information science, computer science, or iSchools (Anderson, 2015, p. 43). ARM programmes are often located in departments that are within schools or faculties such as human science, social science, information science, communication studies, or science. In one case, it is an independent institute within the university. There is no ideal structure. Therefore, this would depend on the peculiarities of the educational institution, as well as national realities.

Professional associations

Professional associations are a critical component of an education system. First, associations may provide a directory or compilation of education and training programmes without endorsing or accrediting them, as demonstrated in Canada and the USA (Association of Canadian Archivists, 2021; Society of American Archivists, 2021). Second, they may monitor and evaluate the content education and training programmes, often providing accreditation for a period, as was the case in Australia, the USA, the UK, and Ireland (Archives and Records Association, 2021; Australian Society of Archivists, 2021). Third, they may guide curriculum development, as demonstrated in the development of graduate curricula in Canada and the USA (Society of American Archivists, 2016).

The state of ARM professional associations is a mixed bag, ranging from a lack of ARM-specific national associations in many countries, to countries having at least one association (Kenya), to others having or having had more than one association (South Africa). In countries that have no national association, ARM professionals have participated in a regional branch of the International Council on Archives, which has three branches in sub-Saharan Africa. One is for east and southern Africa, another for west Africa, and another for central Africa, with north Africa included in the Arab Regional Branch (International Council on Archives, 2021). A unique contribution to ARM education and training was during the 11th biennial meeting of the east and southern regional branch in 1991 where several presentations addressed challenges and opportunities (Kukubo and Seabo, 1992). In 2015, the International Council on Archives launched a five-year African Strategy that identified training and education as one of the two key strategic aims. As part of the programme, the association trained more than half a dozen academics in digital data curatorship (Mojapelo and Ngoepe, 2020, p. 13).

Currently, there are two active national ARM associations, namely the Kenya Association of Records Managers and Archivists and the South African Society of Archivists, as well as a number of intermittently active ones, including the South African Records Management Forum (SARMAF) and the Records and Information Association in Botswana established in 2005 and 2008, respectively (Mojapelo and Ngoepe, 2020, p. 8). However, none of the associations have yet published evidence of having undertaken the three identified contributions to ARM education and training in the form of a directory, evaluation/accreditation, or curriculum development. Nonetheless, they continue to provide other services to the profession, developing a sense of ARM identity and advocacy within the larger society (Mojapelo and Ngoepe, 2020, p. 5).

Conclusion

The outset of this chapter stated the importance of considering each African nation's complex socio-political history, noting great variance between each country and the danger of oversimplification to generalize conclusions for a continent of 54 countries and over a billion people. To this end, the chapter sought, using varied experiences from different countries, to weave the narrative of ARM education and training on the continent. Many of the issues discussed in this chapter are not exclusive to the situation in Africa. For example, relating to the legacy of colonialism, a weak sense of professional identity, and/or debates on theory vs. practical training are issues that the ARM field faces across the world. In response to this, international collaboration has emerged as a proactive approach that allows records professionals to share knowledge and learn from each other.

This chapter adapted a systems thinking approach to explore three categories of issues impacting ARM education: (1) policy and regulatory context; (2) institutional processes and procedures; and (3) stakeholders. The discussion made a deliberate effort to cite copiously, particularly publications from the global south that would otherwise not receive much visibility in global north discussions.

References

Adichie, C. (2009). 'The danger of a single story,' *TED talks*. Available at: www.ted.com/talks/chimamanda_adichie_the_danger_of_a_single_story/transcript?language=en (Accessed 9 August 2021).

African Commission on Human and People's Rights. (2013). *Model law on access to information for Africa*. Available at: www.achpr.org/files/news/2013/04/d84/model_law.pdf (Accessed 9 August 2021).

African Union. (2007). *African charter on democracy, elections and good governance*. Available at: www.right2info.org/resources/publications/instruments-and-standards/africa_charter-on-dem-elections-and-gov_2007_eng (Accessed 8 August 2021).

Ahmadu Bello University. (2021a). *Department of library and information science*. Available at: https://libraryscience.abu.edu.ng/ (Accessed 8 August 2021).

Ahmadu Bello University. (2021b). *LIBS210 Introduction to records and archives management*. Available at: https://moodle.abu.edu.ng/course/info.php?id=2380 (Accessed 9 August 2021).

Ahmadu Bello University. (2021c). *LIBS834 Legal aspects of records and archives.* Available at: https://moodle.abu.edu.ng/course/info.php?id=2455 (Accessed 9 August 2021).

Alexander, P. and Pessek, E. (1988). 'Archives in emerging nations: The Anglophone experience,' *The American Archivist*, 51 (1/2), pp. 120–132.

Anderson, K. (2007). 'Education and training for records professionals,' *Records Management Journal*, 17 (2), pp. 94–106.

Anderson, K. (2015). 'Archival education,' in L. Duranti and P. C. Franks (eds.). *Encyclopedia of archival science*. Lanham, MD: Rowman & Littlefield, pp. 42–46.

Archives and Records Association. (2021). *Careers in records management.* Available at: www.archives.org.uk/careers/careers-in-records-management.html (Accessed 9 August 2021).

ASA and RMAA Joint Education Steering Committee. (2010). *Tasks, competencies & salaries for recordkeeping professionals.* Available at: www.archivists.org.au/documents/item/206 (Accessed 2 August 2021).

Association of Canadian Archivists. (2021). *Graduate archival education in Canada.* Available at: https://archivists.ca/Archival-Education-Programs (Accessed 9 August 2021).

Australian Society of Archivists. (2021). *Accredited courses.* Available at: www.archivists.org.au/learning-publications/accredited-courses (Accessed 9 August 2021).

Bhebhe, S. and Ngoepe, M. (2020). 'Elitism in critical emancipatory paradigm: National archival oral history collection in Zimbabwe and South Africa,' *Archival Science*, 21 (2), pp. 155–172.

Charman, D. and Cook, M. (1967). 'The archives services of East Africa,' *Archives: The Journal of the British Records Association*, 8 (38), pp. 70–80.

Chaterera, F. et al. (2018). *AF03 Investigating the management of digital records in enterprise wide systems: Zimbabwe – final report.* Available at: https://interparestrust.org/assets/public/dissemination/AF03_Draft_FinalReport.pdf (Accessed 8 May 2021).

Chisita, C. T. and Tsabedze, V. W. (2021). 'Massive open online courses (MOOCs): A tool for intercontinental collaboration in archives and records management education in Eswatini,' *Records Management Journal*, 31 (2), pp. 158–175.

Department of Arts and Culture [South Africa]. (2010). *The demand for and supply of skills in library and information services, archival services and records management.* Available at: www.national.archives.gov.za/Final%20Report%2015%20March2010.pdf (Accessed 19 August 2021).

Department of Higher Education and Training [South Africa] and South Africa Qualifications Authority. (2017). *NQF levels and qualifications types.* Available at: https://twitter.com/SAQALive/status/1311023847706103808?s=20 (Accessed 8 August 2021).

Dhukaram, A. V. et al. (2018). 'Higher education provision using systems thinking approach – case studies,' *European Journal of Engineering Education*, 43 (1), pp. 3–25.

Eastern and Southern African Management Institute. (2021). *Faculty.* Available at: https://esami-africa.org/page.php?id=UlU5Uk5ERUU4NTEzNzIyNDc2ODA1MTY xNDA5OQ (Accessed 9 August 2021).

Evans, F. B. (1988). 'The organization and status of archival training: An historical perspective,' *Archivum*, 34, pp. 75–91.
Franks, P. C. (2013). *Records and information management*. Chicago, IL: American Library Association.
Garaba, F. (2015). 'Dodos in the archives: Rebranding the archival profession to meet the challenges of the twenty-first century within ESARBICA,' *Archives and Records: The Journal of the Archives and Records Association*, 36 (2), pp. 216–225.
Gondwe, S. S. (2020). 'Archival education and training opportunities in Malawi: After 50 years, why have we not done well?' in S. M. Keakopa and T. L. Mosweu (eds.). *Cases on electronic record management in the ESARBICA region*. Hershey, PA: IGI Global, pp. 277–297.
Harris, V. (1996). 'Redefining archives in South Africa: Public archives and society in transition, 1990–1996,' *Archivaria*, 1 (42), pp. 6–27.
Hoy, M. (2004). 'Professional development and competency standards: Unravelling the contradictions and maximising opportunities,' *Archives, Memory and Knowledge: The 15th International Congress on Archives*, Vienna, Austria, International Council on Archives.
Institute of Development Management. (2021a). *Business and information resources management – Botswana campus*. Available at: www.idmbls.com/faculty/Business-and-Information-Resource-Management/botswana-campus (Accessed 2 August 2021).
Institute of Development Management. (2021b). *Business and information resources management – Lesotho campus*. Available at: www.idmbls.com/faculty/Business-and-Information-Resource-Management/lesotho-campus (Accessed 2 August 2021).
International Council on Archives. (2021). *ICA regional branches*. Available at: www.ica.org/en/ica-regional-branches.
International Records Management Trust. (2018). *Consultancy projects*. Available at: www.irmt.org/consultancy-services/consultancy-projects-2 (Accessed 9 August 2021).
International Standards Organization. (2019). *ISO/TR 21965 Information and documentation – records management in enterprise architecture*. Available at: www.iso.org/standard/72312.html (Accessed 9 August 2021).
International Standards Organization. (2020). *ISO 16175–1:2020 Information and documentation – processes and functional requirements for software for managing records – part 1: Functional requirements and associated guidance for any applications that manage digital records*. Available at: www.iso.org/standard/74294.html (Accessed 9 August 2021).
Jain, P. and Jorosi, B. N. (2015). 'LIS education in Botswana: A case of DLIS at the University of Botswana,' *IFLA WLIC 2015*. Cape Town, South Africa, IFLA, pp. 1–14.
Jimerson, R. C. (2010). 'From the Pacific Northwest to the global information society: The changing nature of archival education,' *Journal of Western Archives*, 1 (1), pp. 1–22.
Justrell, B. (2007). 'Archives – a prerequisite for democracy: The Swedish national archives training programme in records management for developing countries,' *Swedish Missiological Themes*, 95 (1), pp. 27–36.
Kaffenberger, M. (2021). *Aligning education systems for learning: How systems shift*. Available at: https://riseprogramme.org/blog/aligning-education-systems-for-learning-how-systems-shift (Accessed 21 August 2021).

Kalusopa, T. et al. (2018). *AF04 Enterprise digital records management in Botswana – final report*. Available at: https://interparestrust.org/assets/public/dissemination/AF04_FinalReport_July2018.pdf (Accessed 8 May 2021).

Katuu, S. (2009). 'Archives and records management education and training: What can Africa learn from Europe and North America,' *Information Development*, 25 (2), pp. 133–145.

Katuu, S. (2015). 'The development of archives and records management education and training in Africa – challenges and opportunities,' *Archives and Manuscripts: The Journal of the Australian Society of Archivists*, 43 (2), pp. 96–119.

Katuu, S. (2016). 'Overview of the InterPARES Trust Project in Africa: Trusting records in an increasingly networked environment,' *New Review of Information Networking*, 21 (2), pp. 117–128.

Katuu, S. (2018a). *AF02 managing records in networked environments: South Africa – final report*. Available at: https://interparestrust.org/assets/public/dissemination/AF02FinalReportMarch2018.pdf (Accessed 8 May 2021).

Katuu, S. (2018b). 'The utility of enterprise architecture to records and archives specialists,' in N. Abe et al. (eds.). *2018 IEEE international conference on big data*. Seattle, WA: IEEE, pp. 2702–2710.

Katuu, S. (2019). 'Enterprise architecture – a value proposition for records professionals,' in C. Baru et al. (eds.). *2019 IEEE international conference on big data*. Los Angeles, CA: IEEE, pp. 3116–3125.

Katuu, S. (2020a). 'Enterprise resource planning: Past, present and future,' *New Review of Information Networking*, 25 (1), pp. 37–46.

Katuu, S. (2020b). 'Exploring the challenges facing archives and records professionals in Africa: Historical influences, current developments and opportunities,' in R. Edmondson, L. Jordan and A. C. Prodan (eds.). *The UNESCO memory of the world programme: Key aspects and recent developments*. Cham, Switzerland: Springer Nature, pp. 275–292.

Katuu, S. (2021a). 'Managing records in enterprise resource planning systems,' In Yixin Chen, Heiko Ludwig, Yicheng Tuet al (Eds), *2021 IEEE International Conference on Big Data*, Orlando, FL, IEEE, pp. 2240–2245.

Katuu, S. (2021b). 'Trends in the enterprise resource planning market landscape,' *Journal of Information and Organizational Sciences*, 45 (1), pp. 55–75.

Katuu, S. (2021c). 'Using enterprise architecture in intergovernmental organizations,' In J. Boel and E. Sengsavang (Eds.), *Recordkeeping in International Organizations Archives in Transition in Digital, Networked Environments*. London, Routledge, pp. 154–177.

Katuu, S. and Ngoepe, M. (2015). 'Managing digital records within South Africa's legislative and regulatory framework,' in B. E. Popovsky (ed.). *3rd International conference on cloud security and management ICCSM-2015*. Tacoma, WA: University of Washington, pp. 59–70.

Katuu, S. and Ngoepe, M. (2017). 'Education and training of archives and records management professionals in Africa,' *UNESCO Memory of the World Programme Sub-Committee on Education and Research Newsletter*, 1, pp. 22–27.

Katuu, S. et al. (2018a). *AF01 curriculum alignments at institutions of higher learning in Africa: Preparing professionals to manage records created in networked environments – inventory*. Available at: https://interparestrust.org/assets/public/dissemination/AF01Educationinventory20171.pdf (Accessed 8 May 2021).

Katuu, S. et al. (2018b). *AF01 curriculum alignments at institutions of higher learning in Africa: Preparing professionals to manage records created in networked environments – literature review*. Available at: https://interparestrust.org/assets/public/dissemination/AF01LitReviewJuly2018.pdf (Accessed 8 May 2021).

Katuu, S. et al. (2018c). *AF01 curriculum alignments at institutions of higher learning in Africa: Preparing professionals to manage records created in networked environments – final report*. Available at: https://interparestrust.org/assets/public/dissemination/AF01-FinalReport_1.pdf (Accessed 8 May 2021).

Kenya National Qualifications Authority. (2021a). *Background*. Available at: www.knqa.go.ke/index.php/background/ (Accessed 9 August 2021).

Kenya National Qualifications Authority. (2021b). *Progression pathways*. Available at: www.knqa.go.ke/index.php/progression-pathways/ (Accessed 9 August 2021).

Khayundi, F. (2011). 'Existing records and archival programmes to the job market,' *Journal of the South African Society of Archivists*, 44, pp. 62–73.

Khumalo, N. B. and Chigariro, D. (2017). 'Making a case for the development of a university records and archives management programme at the National University of Science and Technology in Zimbabwe,' *Journal of the South African Society of Archivists*, 50, pp. 67–78.

Kukubo, R. J. W. and Seabo, D. T. (eds.). (1992). 'Archives in the nineties: The challenges for ESARBICA,' *XIth Biennial General Conference*, Gaborone, Botswana, East and Southern Africa Regional Branch of the International Council on Archives.

Lemieux, V. L. and Trapnell, S. E. (2016). *Public access to information for development: A guide to the effective implementation of right to information laws*. Washington DC: World Bank Publications.

Lemieux, V. L. et al. (2019). *Blockchain technology and recordkeeping*. Available at: www.researchgate.net/profile/Victoria_Lemieux/publication/333659272_Blockchain_Technology_Recordkeeping/links/5cfadaaf299bf13a3845866e/Blockchain-Technology-Recordkeeping.pdf (Accessed 9 August 2021).

Lutwama, E. and Kigongo-Bukenya, I. M. N. (2004). 'A tracer study of the East African School of Library and Information Science graduates 1995–1999 working in Uganda,' *South African Journal of Library and Information Science*, 70 (2), pp. 99–109.

Majid, S. (2004). 'Continuing professional development (CPD) activities organized by library and information study programs in Southeast Asia,' *Journal of Education for Library and Information Science*, 45 (1), pp. 58–70.

Marciano, R., S. Agarrat, et al. (2019). 'Reframing digital curation practices through a computational thinking framework,' in C. Baru et al. (eds.). 2019 *IEEE international conference on big data*. Los Angeles, CA: IEEE, pp. 3126–3135.

Marciano, R., V. Lemieux, et al. (2019). 'Establishing an international computational network for librarians and archivists,' *iConference 2019*. Available at: www.ideals.illinois.edu/bitstream/handle/2142/103139/Marciano_et_al_BlueSky2.pdf?sequence=4&isAllowed=y (Accessed 9 August 2021).

Mell, P. and Grance, T. (2011). *The NIST definition of cloud computing*. Gaithersburg, MD: National Institute of Standards and Technology.

Mello, V. M. (2020). *Integrating enterprise resource planning into electronic content management in a South African water utility company*. University of South Africa, Pretoria. PhD thesis.

Moi University. (2021). *Department of library, records management and information studies*. Available at: https://is.mu.ac.ke/index.php/event/lis-ram (Accessed 9 August 2021).

Mojapelo, M. and Ngoepe, M. (2020). 'Advocacy as a strategy to raise the archival profile through the civil society in South Africa,' *Archives and Records*, pp. 1–18.

Moseti, I. et al. (2018). *AF05 enterprise digital records management in Kenya – final report*. Available at: https://interparestrust.org/assets/public/dissemination/AF05FinalReportMarch2018.pdf (Accessed 8 May 2021).

Mosweu, T., Mosweu, O. and Luthuli, L. (2019). 'Implications of cloud-computing services in records management in Africa: Achilles heels of the digital era?' *South African Journal of Information Management*, 21 (1), pp. 1–12.

National University of Science and Technology. (2021). *Department of records and archives management*. Available at: www.nust.ac.zw/cis/index.php/departments/records-archives-management (Accessed 9 August 2021).

Nengomasha, C. T. (2006). 'Training for the archival profession in Namibia,' *Archival Science*, 6 (2), pp. 205–218.

Ngoepe, M. (2008). *An exploration of records management trends in the South African public sector: A case study of the Department of Provincial and Local Government*. Department of Information Science. University of South Africa, Pretoria. Master's thesis.

Ngoepe, M., Jacobs, L. and Mojapelo, M. (2022). 'Inclusion of digital records in the archives and records management curricula in a comprehensive open distance e-learning environment,' *Information Development*. Doi:10.1177/02666669221081812.

Ngoepe, M. and Katuu, S. (2017). 'Provision of records created in networked environments in the curricula of institutions of higher learning in Africa,' *New Review of Information Networking*, 22 (1), pp. 1–12.

Ngoepe, M., Maluleka, J. and Onyancha, B. (2014). 'Research collaboration in the archives and records management field across and beyond universities in Africa: An informetric analysis,' *Mousaion: South African Journal for Information Studies*, 32 (3), pp. 119–135.

Ngoepe, M. and Saurombe, N. (2021). 'Africanisation of the South African archival curriculum: A preliminary study of undergraduate courses in an open distance e-learning environment,' *Education for Information*, 37 (1), pp. 53–68.

Nnamdi Azikiwe University. (2021). *Library and information science programmes*. Available at: https://education.unizik.edu.ng/dept/library-and-information-science/library-and-information-science-programmes/ (Accessed 9 August 2021).

Noko, P. and Ngulube, P. (2015). 'A vital feedback loop in educating and training archival professionals: A tracer study of records and archives management graduates in Zimbabwe,' *Information Development*, 31 (3), pp. 270–283.

Organisation of African Unity. (1981). *African charter on human and peoples' rights*. Available at: https://au.int/sites/default/files/treaties/36390-treaty-0011_-_african_charter_on_human_and_peoples_rights_e.pdf (Accessed 20 July 2021).

Rieger, M. (1972). 'Archives in developing countries: The regional training center movement,' *The American Archivist*, 35 (2), pp. 163–171.

Right2Info. (2021). *Constitutional provisions, laws and regulations*. Available at: www.right2info.org/laws/constitutional-provisions-laws-and-regulations (Accessed 8 August 2021).

Schaeffer, R. C. (1997). *The knowledge-base and archival professionalism in North America: A political history*. University of British Columbia, Vancouver, BC. Master's thesis.

Shepherd, E. (2012). 'An 'academic' dilemma: The tale of archives and records management,' *Journal of Librarianship and Information Science*, 44 (3), pp. 174–184.

Society of American Archivists. (2016). *Guidelines for a graduate program in archival studies*. Available at: https://www2.archivists.org/prof-education/graduate/gpas (Accessed 2 August 2021).

Society of American Archivists. (2021). *Directory for archival education*. Available at: https://www2.archivists.org/dae (Accessed 9 August 2021).

Technical University of Kenya. (2021). *List of programmes – department of information and knowledge management*. Available at: http://sics.tukenya.ac.ke/index.php/courses-in-the-department (Accessed 9 August 2021).

Theron, J. C. (1998). 'Proposed education of archivists at the University of South Africa,' *South African Archives Journal*, 40, pp. 110–117.

Thurston, A. (1985). 'The training of archivists from developing countries: A Commonwealth perspective,' *Archivaria*, 20, pp. 116–126.

Tough, A. G. (2009). 'Archives in sub-Saharan Africa half a century after independence,' *Archival Science*, 9 (3–4), pp. 187–201.

Tough, A. G. (2012). 'Oral culture, written records and understanding the twentieth-century colonial archive. The significance of understanding from within,' *Archival Science*, 12 (3), pp. 245–265.

Université Cheikh Anta Diop de Dakar. (2021a). *Admission to the first year of the license (face-to-face)*. Available at: https://ebad.ucad.sn/?q=content/admission-en-premi%C3%A8re-ann%C3%A9e-de-la-licence-en-pr%C3%A9sentiel (Accessed 9 August 2021).

Université Cheikh Anta Diop de Dakar. (2021b). *Admission to the first year of the master (face-to-face or distance learning)*. Available at: https://ebad.ucad.sn/?q=content/admission-en-premi%C3%A8re-ann%C3%A9e-du-master-pr%C3%A9sentielle-ou-distancielle (Accessed 9 August 2021).

University of Botswana. (2021). *Department of library and information studies*. Available at: www.ub.bw/discover/faculties/humanities/library-and-information-studies (Accessed 9 August 2021).

University of Ghana. (2021). *Department of information studies – brief history*. Available at: www.ug.edu.gh/infostudies/about/brief_history (Accessed 9 August 2021).

University of Ibadan. (2021a). *Academic programme: faculty of education*. Available at: www.ui.edu.ng/accademicedu (Accessed 9 August 2021).

University of Ibadan. (2021b). *History: Department of library, archival and information studies*. Available at: https://educ.ui.edu.ng/history-department-library-archival-and-information-studies (Accessed 9 August 2021).

University of Namibia. (2021). *Department of information and communication studies*. Available at: www.unam.edu.na/faculty-of-humanities-and-social-sciences/information-and-communication-studies (Accessed 9 August 2021).

University of South Africa. (2021a). *Department of information science – new qualification*. Available at: www.unisa.ac.za/sites/corporate/default/Colleges/Human-Sciences/Schools,-departments,-centres,-institutes-&-units/School-of-Arts/Department-of-Information-Science/New-Qualification (Accessed 9 August 2021).

University of South Africa. (2021b). *Honours degrees and postgraduate diplomas*. Available at: www.unisa.ac.za/sites/corporate/default/Apply-for-admission/Honours-degrees-&-postgraduate-diplomas/Qualifications/All-qualifications (Accessed 9 August 2021).

University of South Africa. (2021c). *Masters and doctoral degrees*. Available at: www.unisa.ac.za/sites/corporate/default/Apply-for-admission/Master%27s-&-doctoral-degrees/Qualifications/All-qualifications (Accessed 9 August 2021).

Zimbabwe Open University. (2021). *Department of information science and records management*. Available at: www.zou.ac.zw/faculty_of_applied_social_sciences/department-information-science-and-records-management (Accessed 9 August 2021).

Epilogue

Mpho Ngoepe

In the African context, this book interrogated interrelated themes in the domains of legislation, infrastructure, authentication, trust, and education in digital records. The content on these areas draws from the InterPARES trust's research conducted by the Africa Team. The project's outcomes were central to:

- empowerment of master's and doctoral students, which resulted in two PhD graduates;
- curriculum development and review in digital records at several African universities, including the University of South Africa, the University of Namibia, and the University of Eswatini (Ngoepe and Saurombe, 2021);
- providing the foundation for the International Council on Archives' Africa strategy, especially in the areas of archival education and training (Lowry, 2017);
- results relevant to the African setting and empowerment of archives repositories (as practitioners were involved); and
- achievement of action-oriented outcomes (for example, guidelines and checklists for authenticating digital records to support the audit process).

Overall, the project outcomes are classified into three categories: scholarly benefits (knowledge creation, research collaboration, and enhanced curriculum), social benefits (enhanced policy, professional practice, and legal outcomes), and audiences (the public, archives repositories, and government).

The chapters make it clear that reliable records are important evidence of actions taken and decisions made by public officials, allowing the government to account for its actions or stakeholders in the case of the private sector. The reliability of such records is determined by a variety of factors, including the legislative framework, infrastructure, technology, and

DOI: 10.4324/9781003203155-7

Epilogue 129

people in charge of managing such records. A reliable record is one that is capable of standing up to the evidence that it confirms. The chapters laid a solid foundation for the effective management of digital records to ensure accountability, transparency, and good governance in an ever-changing world for the betterment of citizens' lives. This has been demonstrated through discussions about archival legislation, infrastructure, authentication, trust, and education.

Except for South Africa, most African countries enacted archival legislation shortly after their independence, often modelled after the United Kingdom's Public Record Act of 1958 or former colonial masters, such as Portugal in Mozambique and Angola. From Chapter 1, it is clear that these pieces of legislation were mostly written with paper records in mind, while remaining silent on records in other media, such as digital media. Although Chapter 1 only focused on four countries, literature suggests that most African countries operate national archival systems under outdated or incomplete legislation, or even without any legislation at all, such as Zambia (1964), Lesotho (1967), Malawi (1975, amended in 1989), and Eswatini (1971), to name a few. The situation is exacerbated by the fact that, despite the large mandate placed on the institutions, archival legislation in some countries has never been costed. As a result, these institutions' only budgets are for salaries and training, while line function activities are neglected.

With the outbreak of the COVID-19 pandemic, which has forced millions of people worldwide to work from remote locations using technology, organizations experienced challenges in providing employees with access to authentic and legally admissible records to support their functions. Such challenges include organizations' inability to maintain the authenticity of digital records because, unlike physical records, they are easily corrupted, resulting in digital records losing their trustworthiness credence. The information in the chapters challenges professionals such as information technology specialists and records managers to review, rethink, and recalibrate their digital systems, as well as internal policies, to ensure they can be used just as effectively from home as they can in the office, while also ensuring the integrity and reliability of their organizations' records.

Digital records infrastructure provides foundational tools and services that are required to unlock acceptable records management practices of records held in digital spaces and electronic environments. Chapter 2 revealed that the vast majority of those responsible for managing digital assets and records are unfamiliar with and sceptical of digital records infrastructure such as enterprise content management (ECM) systems and enterprise resource planning (ERP) systems. As a result, the level of infrastructure implementation and integration is very low, depicting a missed opportunity for countries to move towards e-government. Nonetheless, Chapter 4 highlighted the significance of capitalizing on their respective governments' apparent willingness to undertake public sector structural reforms, emphasizing the importance of establishing digital records infrastructure to ensure that digital records provide evidence and authenticity that support open and e-government initiatives.

From the audit perspective, the value of auditing is in its ability to provide an independent assurance of the usefulness and reliability of accounting information, which promotes efficient, economic, and effective use of public resources. To produce effective reports, audit institutions depend on source evidence found in official records that document the business actions of the institutions being audited. As such, effective records management forms the basis for financial management systems and, subsequently, supports evidence for audits. It is critical for auditors to understand that the digital chain of custody must always be maintained to support the authenticity of digital records. Ensuring the integrity and reliability of digital records necessitates an understanding of various aspects, which both Chapters 3 and 4 provided. Chapter 3 explored the development of guidelines that auditors can use as is or adapt to judge the authenticity of digital records wherever records must be relied on as trustworthy evidence to support the audit process. In this regard, auditors can audit organizations that have implemented ECM and ERP systems remotely. This can be made even easier if such systems are integrated.

The scarcity of archival training programmes in Africa is one of the root causes of the problems identified previously. As discussed in Chapter 5, the number of students who qualify for these programmes is very small, and it may be difficult for institutions of higher learning to sustain these programmes in the long run. This is evident in the inventory of training institutions in 38 of Africa's 54 countries, which includes only a few archival programmes. When it comes to archival associations, the situation is even worse. As argued in Chapter 5, the only known active archival associations in Africa are the South African Society of Archivists and the Kenya Association of Records Managers and Archivists at the national level, and the Eastern and Southern Regional Branch of the International Council on Archives (ESARBICA) at the regional level. While the Records and Information Association of Botswana exists in name, it is dormant to this day.

Finally, the chapters in this book provided the opportunity for better insights into the management of digital records in Africa, as well as the challenges that remain imprinted on the conscience of all stakeholders who cherish, uphold, and unflinchingly defend the principles of effective records management amidst the seismic shifts in the dynamic infosphere realm. It is hoped that the book will leave an indelible mark on the scholarly and professional discourse and praxis of effective records management in both the private and public sectors, drawing on the contributions of effulgent experts and budding scholars in information management, archives, and records management.

References

Lowry, J. (2017). 'A report on education and training in the International Council on Archives' Africa Programme,' *Education for Information*, 33 (2), pp. 107–119.

Ngoepe, M. and Saurombe, N. (2021). 'Africanisation of the South African archival curriculum: A preliminary study of undergraduate courses in an open distance e-learning environment,' *Education for Information*, 37 (1), pp. 53–68.

Annexure A
Guidelines for authenticating digital records to support the audit process

1. Assessment of the general control environment of the auditee

It is important to first assess the information systems environment in which the electronic document management system (EDMS), enterprise resource planning (ERP) system, or other information system operates to determine whether reliance can be placed on the general controls surrounding the system. It is therefore important to request the information systems auditors to include this system as part of their general controls review of the auditee.

2. Assessment of the electronic document management system controls of the auditee

After the general control environment of the auditee has been assessed and the key internal controls found to be operating effectively, the EDMS authentication checklist should be completed to assess the authenticity and reliability of the digital records that are stored or created on the EDMS, ERP system, or other relevant information systems. The checklist has been divided into the focus described in the table that follows.

FOCUS AREA	SUB-FOCUS AREAS	OBJECTIVE OF SUB-FOCUS AREA
Controls required for digital records	System validations	Validation of systems to ensure accuracy, reliability, consistent intended performance, and the ability to discern altered invalid records.
	Record inspection	The ability to generate accurate and complete copies of records in both human readable and digital form suitable for inspection, review, and copying by the public audit oversight system such as the Auditor General of South Africa (AGSA).
	Record protection	Protection of records to enable their accurate and ready retrieval throughout the records retention period.
	Security	Limiting system access to authorized individuals.
	Audit trail	Use of secure, computer-generated, time-stamped audit trails to independently record the date and time of operator entries and actions that create, modify, or delete digital records. Record changes shall not obscure previously recorded information. Such audit trail documentation shall be retained for a period at least as long as that required for the subject digital records and shall be available for AGSA's review and copying.
	Authority check	Use of authority checks to ensure that only authorized individuals can use the system, electronically sign a record, access the operation or computer system input or output device, alter a record, or perform the operation at hand.
	Accountability and responsibility for actions	The establishment of, and adherence to, written policies that hold individuals accountable and responsible for actions initiated under their electronic signatures, in order to deter record and signature falsifications.
	System documentation controls	Use of appropriate controls over systems documentation including: (1) adequate controls over the distribution of, access to, and use of documentation for system operation and maintenance; and (2) revision and change control procedures to maintain an audit trail that documents time-sequenced development and modification of systems documentation.

(Continued)

FOCUS AREA	SUB-FOCUS AREAS	OBJECTIVE OF SUB-FOCUS AREA
	Signing requirements	Signed electronic records should contain information associated with the signing that clearly indicates all of the following: (1) the printed name of the signer; (2) the date and time when the signature was executed; and (3) the meaning (such as review, approval, responsibility, or authorship) associated with the signature.
Controls required for electronic signatures	Linking signatures to digital records	Electronic signatures and handwritten signatures executed to digital records shall be linked to their respective electronic records to ensure that the signatures cannot be excised, copied, or otherwise transferred to falsify a digital record by ordinary means.
	Uniqueness of signature	Each electronic signature shall be unique to one individual and shall not be reused by, or reassigned to, anyone else.
	Verification of identifies	Before an organization establishes, assigns, certifies, or otherwise sanctions an individual's electronic signature, or any element of such electronic signature, the organization shall verify the identity of the individual.
	Electronic signature components and controls	Electronic signatures that are not based upon biometrics should: (1) Employ at least two distinct identification components such as an identification code and password. (i) When an individual executes a series of signings during a single, continuous period of controlled system access, the first signing should be executed using all electronic signature components; subsequent signings should be executed using at least one electronic signature component that is only executable by, and designed to be used only by, the individual. (ii) When an individual executes one or more signings not performed during a single, continuous period of controlled system access, each signing should be executed using all the following electronic signature components: (a) be used only by their genuine owners; and (b) be administered and executed to ensure that attempted use of an individual's electronic signature by anyone other than its genuine owner requires collaboration of two or more individuals.

Monitoring of IDs and Passwords	It should be ensured that identification codes and passwords issued are periodically monitored, recalled, or revised. Where identification and/or password tokens are used, loss management procedures to electronically deauthorize lost, stolen, missing, or otherwise potentially compromised tokens, cards, and other devices that bear or generate identification codes or password information, and to issue temporary or permanent replacements using suitable, rigorous controls, should exist.

Annexure A

The outcome of the assessments performed on the EDMS authentication checklist will determine the reliance that can be placed by regularity auditors on controls within the EDMS, ERP system, or other information systems, and thereby the impact of risks on the class of transactions, account balances, or disclosures which need to be tested. To make an overall conclusion based on the outcome of the checklist, the guidance in the table that follows can be used.

OVERALL CHECKLIST CONCLUSION	IMPACT ON RISK OF CLASS OF TRANSACTIONS, ACCOUNT BALANCE, OR DISCLOURES	IMPACT OF CONCLUSION
Intervention required	Significant risk	Reliance can be placed on the general information technology (IT) controls, but the system controls relating to authenticity are not adequate.
Concerning	Standard risk	Reliance can be placed on the general IT controls, but concerns exist relating to the system controls in ensuring that authenticity can be derived, which need to be addressed.
Good	Minimal risk	Reliance can be placed on the general IT controls as well as on the system controls in that a presumption of authenticity can be derived.

Index

Note: Page numbers in *italic* indicate a figure and page numbers in **bold** indicate a table on the corresponding page

Access to Information Act (Kenya) 16–17, 31–34, 94–95
Access to Information and Protection of Privacy Act (AIPPA) 35–36
access to information (ATI) laws 16–17, 28–36, 94–95; and ARM profession 36–37
Africa: archival training centres 101; archives education and training 99–120; authentication of records 71–86; data protection 43–44; digital records infrastructure 49–70; law and recordkeeping 7–48; professional associations in 119–120; trust in digital records 89; trustworthiness of records 87–98; *see also* specific African nations
AGSA *see* Auditor General of South Africa (AGSA)
AIPPA *see* Access to Information and Protection of Privacy Act (AIPPA)
Alphabet 43
archives: and colonialism 18–19; education and training for 99–120, 130; *see also* recordkeeping
archives and records management (ARM): continuing professional development in 114–115; curriculum development 109–110; educational institutions for 118–119; educators for 116–118; policy and regulatory context 108–109; professional institutions in 119–120; qualifications or specializations

113–114; research in 113; students in 118; technology competences in 111–113; theory *vs.* practical training 110–111; training and education 99–120, 130
archivists and training 3–4, 99–120, 130
ARM *see* archives and records management (ARM)
auditing records 71–84, 130; guidelines for 80–83, **82**, 132–136; logs 81; process 78–80, 130; trails in authentication of records 77; trustworthiness of digital records 77–80
Auditor General of South Africa (AGSA) 71, 78
authentication of records 3, 20, 25, 71–84, 88; assessment guidelines 80–83, **82**; legislative framework and standards 73–76; risks affecting 76–77

Banking (Credit Reference Bureau) Regulations, 2013 38
Bechuanaland *see* Botswana
binding precedent 14
blockchain technology 72, 77, 112
Botswana: and access to information (ATI) laws 30–31; cloud computing deployment 59–64, *60*, *62*; constitutional right of access 12; data protection laws 37–38; digital infrastructure deployment *56*, 57–59,

59; digital infrastructure of 52–53;
education for archives and records
102; and electronic land management
information systems 91; enterprise
resource planning (ERP) system
deployment 64, *65*, **66**, 67; and
Government Data Network (GDN)
90–91; having mixed legal systems
8–10, **9**; national archives and laws
of 19–20, 24; and trustworthiness
of digital records 89–91; use of
enterprise content management
systems 90–91
Botswana Land Integrated System
(BLISL) 91
Botswana National Archives and
Records Services (BNARS) 19, 90
British South Africa Company 11, 25

case law 12–14
Central African Archives 26
Central African Federation (CAF) 26
checksum 72, 77
civil law 10
cloud computing 49, 50, 51, 52, 53,
90, 111–112; deployment 59–61,
60; deployment model 61–64, *63*;
service models 61, *62*; types 54–55
colonialism 100; data 43–44; shaping
law system 8, 11, 15, 18–19
common law systems 12
community cloud computing 54
computer assisted audit techniques
(CAATs) 79
constitutionalism 11–12
constitution as source of law 11–12
Constitution of Zimbabwe
Amendment 35
continuing professional development
in archives and records management
(ARM) 114–115
County Governments Act 34
Court Records Management System
(CRMS) 91
COVID-19 and auditing 79, 83, 129
curriculum development in education
for archives and records 109–110
customary law 14–15
customer relationship management
(CRM) 112

Cybercrime and Computer Related
Crimes Act 31
Cyber Security and Data Protection
Bill, 2019 42

data colonialism 43–44
data privacy 36, 38, 41–42
data protection 37–43; and data
colonialism 43–44
Data Protection Act, 2018
(Botswana) 37
Data Protection Act (Kenya) 38–40, 43
data surveillance 39
digital chain of custody 72–73,
130
digital diplomatics 88
Digital Economy Blueprint
(Kenya) 52
digital infrastructure 49–68, 129–130
digital records 20; auditing 78–80;
authentication 3, 20, 25, 71–84;
background 1–2; in Botswana 20;
integrity of 88–89; in Kenya 22–23;
trustworthiness of 72–73, 77–80
Document Management Workflow
System (DMWS) 91

Eastern and Southern African
Management Institute (ESAMI) 102,
103, 108
Eastern and Southern Regional Branch
of the International Council on
Archives (ESARBICA) 55, 130
ECM system *see* enterprise content
management (ECM) system
EDRMS *see* electronic document
record management system
(EDRMS)
educational institutions for archives
and records management (ARM)
118–119
education for archives and records
99–120; history of 100–102;
institutional processes and
procedures 109–115; stakeholders
115–120
education system and systems thinking
approach 108–120
educators in archives and records
management (ARM) 116–118

Index 139

Electronic Communication and Transaction Act (ECTA) (No. 25 of 2002) 74, 79, 80, 91
Electronic Communication and Transactions Act (No. 14 of 2014) 20, 89
electronic document record management system (EDRMS) 50, 53
Electronic Evidence (Records) Act (No. 13 of 2014) 20, 89
electronic records *see* digital records
Electronic Records (Evidence) Act (No. 13 of 2014) 89
electronic signatures 77, 80, 90, 134
English common law 8, 10
enterprise architecture 112–113
enterprise content management (ECM) system 49, 51, 52–53, 55, 94, 96, 129; definition 90; deployment 56, 56–58; and trustworthy records 89
enterprise resource planning (ERP) system 49, 53, 54, 79, 112, 129; deployment 56, 56–58, 64–67, 65, **66**
ERP *see* enterprise resource planning (ERP) system
Eswatini and education for archives and records 102–103

Facebook 43
freedom of information (FOI) laws *see* access to information (ATI) laws

Ghana and education for archives and records 103
Government Data Network (GDN) 90–91
government stakeholders for archives and records 115–116

higher education qualifications in education for archives and records 115–116
hybrid cloud computing 54

ICT 52, 89, 90, 94
indigenous law 14–15
information and communications technology *see* ICT

information archaeology 92
information architecture 92
Institute of Development Management (IDM) 102
Intelligence and Security Services Act 31
International Council of Archives (ICA) 55, 88, 119
International Project on Permanent Authentic Records in Electronic Systems Trust project *see* InterPARES project
International Records Management Trust (IRMT) 116–117
International Standards on Auditing (ISAs) 80–81
InterPARES project 1, 2, 88, 99, 113, 117, 128
Islamic law 15–16

jurisdiction in law systems 12–13

Kadhi's courts 15
Kenya: and access to information (ATI) laws 31–34; cloud computing deployment 60, 60–64, 61, 62; constitutional law 12; court structure 12–13, 13; data protection laws 38–39; digital infrastructure deployment 56, 57–59, 59; digital infrastructure of 52; education for archives and records 103–104; enterprise resource planning (ERP) system deployment 64, 65, **66**, 67; having mixed legal systems 9, **9**; higher education qualifications 115–116; Islamic law in 15–16; legislation and archives and records management (ARM) 108; national archives and laws of 20–23; and trustworthiness of digital records 94–96
Kenya Association of Records Managers and Archivists 119, 130
Kenya Information and Communications Act, 2009 22, 23, 38
Kenya National Archives and Documentation Service 21–22
Kenya Qualifications Authority (KNQA) 115

140 Index

Land Inventory for Tribal Land Boards of Botswana (LYNSIS) 91
land management information systems 91
law case 12–14
law(s): access to information (ATI) laws 16–17, 28–36, 94–95; civil 10; common law systems 12; customary and indigenous 14–15; data protection 37–43; hierarchy of *16*, 16–36; impact of colonialism 8, 11, 15; interpretation and enforcement of 17–18; Islamic 15–16; mixed legal systems 8–9, **9**; national archives law 19–28; omnibus 12; personal 10; private 10; public 10; and record keeping 3, 7–44; sectoral 12; sources of 10–16; statutes and regulations 12; as a system 7–11
law system impacted by colonialism 8, 11, 15, 18–19
Law Trust Part Services (Pty) Ltd 80
legislation and archives and records management (ARM) 108–109, 129
Lesotho and education for archives and records 104

Malawi and education for archives and records 104–105
Media Practitioners Act 31
metadata: in auditing 81; and authentication of records 77; for integrity 89
mixed legal systems 8–9, **9**

Namibia and education for archives and records 105
National Archives Act 16, 35
national archives and laws 19–28, 75, 93–94
National Archives and Records Management System (NARMS) 52, 90–91
National Archives and Records Service of South Africa Act (NARS Act) 19–20, 23–25, 75
National Archives and Records Service of South Africa (NARSSA) 75
National Archives of Rhodesia 25–26

National Archives of Zimbabwe 25–26, *26*, 50
National Archives of Zimbabwe Act 27–28, 93–94
National Intelligence Service (NIS) Act 39
National Qualification Framework (NQF) 115, *116*
National Security Act (Botswana) 31
Nigeria and education for archives and records 105

Official Secrets Act, Cap. 187 39
omnibus laws 12
Organization of African Unity 108–109
Oscar Pistorius versus the State of South Africa 77

PAIA *see* Promotion of Access to Information Act (PAIA)
personal information, defined 33
personal law 10
persuasive precedent 14
platform as a service (PaaS) model 63
policy stakeholders in education for archives and records 115–116
POPI Act *see* Protection of Personal Information Act (POPI Act)
Prevention of Terrorism Act (2012) 39
private law 10
professional associations in archives and records management (ARM) 119–120, 130
Promotion of Access to Information Act (PAIA) 34–35
Protection of Personal Information Act (POPI Act) 39–41
Public Archives and Documentation Service Act (Kenya) 21, 96
Public Audit Act (South Africa) 78
public cloud computing 54
public law 10
Public Order and Security Act (POSA) 36

Rand Water 51
recordkeeping: and law 3, 7–48; *see also* archives
Records and Information Association 119

Index 141

Records Management in Service of Democracy (RMSD) programme 114
regulations and archives and records management (ARM) 108–109
research in archives and records management (ARM) 113
right to information laws *see* access to information (ATI) laws
Roman-Dutch law 8–9, 10

SANS 15801 75, 82
sectoral laws 12
Security Laws (Amendment) Act, 2014 39
Senegal and education for archives and records 106
shariah see Islamic law
social media records 76
software as a service (SaaS) model 62–63
South Africa: and access to information (ATI) laws 34–35; auditing records 78–79; authentication of records 74–76; cloud computing deployment 59–64, *60*, *62*; constitutional right of access 12; data protection laws 39–41; digital infrastructure deployment 56, 57–59, *59*; digital infrastructure of 51; education for archives and records 106–107; enterprise resource planning (ERP) system deployment 64, *65*, **66**, 67; having mixed legal systems 8–10, **9**; higher education qualifications 115, *116*; national archives and laws of 2325; and trustworthiness of digital records 91–93
South African Post Office Ltd 80
South African Records Management Forum (SARMAF) 119
South African Society of Archivists 119, 130
Southern Rhodesia *see* Zimbabwe

stakeholders in education for archives and records 115–120
stare decisis 12
State Land Information Management System (SLIMS) 91
statutes and regulations 12
students in archives and records management (ARM) 118
supply chain management (SCM) 112
systems thinking approach to education system 108–120

Tanzania and education for archives and records 102, 103
Team Africa 1, 2, 128
technology in archives and records management (ARM) 111–113
training, theory vs practical 110–111
training for archives and records 3–4, 99–120, 130
Tribal Land Information Management System (TLIMS) 91
trustworthiness of digital records 72–73, 77–80, 87–97

UNESCO and training in archives and records management 101
University of South Africa 106–107, 109–110, 114, 117

Zimbabwe 59–64, *60*, *62*; and access to information (ATI) laws 35–36; data protection laws 41–43; digital infrastructure deployment 56, 57–59, *59*; digital infrastructure of 50; education for archives and records 107–108; enterprise resource planning (ERP) system deployment 64, *65*, **66**, 67; having mixed legal systems 8–9, **9**, 10–11; national archives and laws of 25–28; and trustworthiness of digital records 93–94

For Product Safety Concerns and Information please contact our EU representative GPSR@taylorandfrancis.com
Taylor & Francis Verlag GmbH, Kaufingerstraße 24, 80331 München, Germany

www.ingramcontent.com/pod-product-compliance
Lightning Source LLC
Chambersburg PA
CBHW051750230426
43670CB00012B/2225